the
anxious hippie

the
anxious hippie

from worry, fear, & overreacting
to finding the peace, love,
& blessings in anxiety

LUCIE DICKENSON

THE ANXIOUS HIPPIE

Published by Inspired Girl Books
821 Belmar Plaza, Unit 5 Belmar, NJ 07719
www.inspiredgirlbooks.com

Inspired Girl Books is honored to bring forth books with heart and stories that matter. We are proud to offer this book to our readers; the story, the experiences, and the words are the author's alone.

ISBN: 978-1-7350944-0-3

Cover design and typesetting by Roseanna White Designs
Cover illustration by Shutterstock
Author photograph by Gorden Dickenson

Library of Congress Control Number:
2020910612

Contents

Acknowledgements...9

Author's Note...13

Foreword..15

Introduction..17

Part 1

Taking It In..19

1: And The Award Goes To 21

2: Soap Tastes Awful 23

3: Playing House..27

4: Crank Up The Tunes..29

5: Don't Pass Notes in School, Dear 32

6: School Is For Learning...36

7: Family And Food Perfect Together..............................38

8: Baked Ziti..40

9: Let The Sun Shine...42

10: How About Some Sugar, Sugar? 44

11: The Reaction...47

12: Love? 50

13: What's That Smell?...52

14: Come Home from the Party Please 54

15: If This Is Help, No Thank You................................57

16: Really Where Is the Italian Food?............................59

17: There Is Always Laughter.....................................61

18: Home. Less...63

19: Love Does Exist 65

Part 2

Going Within 67

20: My Baby And Me 69

21: That Will Be One Hundred Fifty Dollars....74

22: What's Your Emergency? 79

23: What I Planted, Grew 83

24: The Vampire..87

25: My Comedy Act.....................................91

26: The Great Purge 93

27: Energy is My New Buzzword.........................94

28: Shutting Shit Down.................................97

29: Road Trip...102

30: The Gas Guy.......................................106

31: What Is Safe? 109

32: Hot Mess...112

33: Over The Bridge 118

34: I Am a Super Hero 122

35: Operation Stink Eye...............................126

36: It's Happening!...................................130

37: The Pirate's Life for Me 133

38: The Anxiety Trick.................................138

39: Bottoms Up 141

40: Tick-Tock...145

41: I Am Not Cooking..................................149

42: The Waxed Woman...................................153

43: The School 157

44: Stop the World, I Want to Get Off.........160

45: The Hospital Loop.................................164

46: The Lollipop Guild 167

47: Another Dimension 171

48: Drink Up..175

49: Intruder Alert 177

50: That's Amore......................................181

51: Seeing the Light..................................184

52: Dreaming Awake..187
53: A Quick Jaunt..192
54: Two for the Price of One..................195
55: Role Reversal...199
56: Wheels Up...204
57: A New Perspective 209

Part 3

The Lessons...217
58: I know. I know. Not Self-Help. 219
59: Take a Detour 222
60: Crowd Out...224
61: Fear or Love..227
62: Good Morning.......................................229
63: I Am Me 231
64: Say Hello to My Little Friend.....................233
65: There is Enough.....................................235
66: Secrets Make You Sick 237
67: New Energy 239
68: The Happy Train.....................................242
69: Take Out the Garbage 244
70: Law of Thirds...246
71: Going Fishing? 248
72: Acceptance 251
73: God Has Got This...................................253
74: These Thoughts......................................256
75: It's in the Genes.....................................258
76: Groundhog Day 260
77: There's a Party in my Tummy 262
78: Get Outside and Go 264
79: Setbacks...266
80: Imperfect 268

81: Sharing Your Smile 271
82: Why the Name? 273
83: The Anxious Hippie 276

Part 4

Peace of Mind 279
84: Now You Know 281
About the Author 287

Acknowledgements

Thank you to Jenn Tuma-Young who knew what I needed to write before I did. Her guidance and experience were not just helpful, but instrumental in writing this book. Thank you for being such an incredible publisher and friend. To Jessica Varion-Carroll for telling me more than once that I needed to talk to Jennifer about publishing. To Roseanna White, Janelle Leonard, and Jessica Morrisy for being part of my team. I am so grateful for you all.

To my kids: Sean, Kate and Colleen. You have taught me so many lessons along the way. Thank you for picking me to be your mother. You each are such incredible humans. I cannot even contain my excitement for what is to come for each of you in the future.

And to Gordon. What can I say? I told you it was going to be a wild ride. I wouldn't change one single thing. You have been such a support, a friend and an incredible husband. Thank you for being you. I fall in love with you a little more every day.

⚠ **WARNING:**

THIS BOOK IS NOT WRITTEN COMFORTABLY. There are fractured sentences. There are run-on sentences. There are punctuation problems. There is word diarrhea. There is word omission. You may even experience rapid heartbeat while reading these short chapters. All of it purposefully. I tried my best to get you on the inside of the mind and the skin of someone suffering with anxiety and chemical sensitivities.

Author's Note

ALTHOUGH THE BOOK LIGHTLY FOLLOWS A chronological order, events may be out of sequence. I could not possibly fit into a book all I did to heal and all the stories that happened on my journey. At no time is this book stating that one story followed the other. I also chose to keep the privacy of many people and as such may have changed their identifying features. Many of the conversations I have in this book have been re-created to the best of my knowledge and memory. Because we all have our own perspective in growing up and how we see things, my story may be different from someone else's version . . . but yeah, this stuff happened and it may sound absolutely cray-cray, but it's true.

This book is my story. It is meant to be motivational and informative. This book is not meant to be used, nor should be used, to diagnose or treat any medical condition. For diagnosis or treatment of any medical issue, please consult your own physician. The doctors and treatments that I used were for my own benefit and not meant to be an endorsement or recommendation for any service. The author and publisher are not liable for any damages or negative consequences from any treatment, action, application or preparation for anyone reading or following the story and information in this book.

P.S.- My way is not your way anyway. We all have a unique road to follow. Follow your way.

P.P.S.- This is just a segment of my life. This story focuses on the anxiety. There is so much more to me than this, however this is the piece of my life I chose to tell.

Foreword

I KNEW I WAS IN FOR AN ADVENTURE LIKE NO other pretty early on.

I was changing a tire on the side of the parkway during rush hour, and I see a flash of orange out of the corner of my eye. It was my girlfriend, of only a couple of weeks. She was wearing the emergency kit orange poncho, doing a cheer routine on the side of the road. She was trying to get me to laugh. Mission accomplished Lucie.

Fast forward to today and I am intimidated by being asked to write the foreword to a very personal and powerful book. I'm an avid reader, not a writer. How can I or anyone else do this book justice? It's a deeply personal recounting of a very difficult time in the author's life. A time where she was seeking help and insight on the very edge of healing science. Help that was needed for an anxiety condition that had taken root many years ago. The anxiety grew alongside of her and had at times, crippled her. Let me say this though, at no time did she give up despite how terrible some years were.

Her story is one of courage and determination. Chasing the light at the end of the tunnel and eventually finding that light within, where it was all along. I was a witness to many of the stories in this book, and I was almost arrested in one. I saw a healthy young woman struggle so much that she lost 50 pounds despite the two-thousand calorie breakfasts I would make her. I saw her struggle socially, struggle with OCD and many other not so fun things. Through it all the fire in her eyes never went out, it blazed hard with fierce bravery radiating from her beautiful brown eyes. I am in awe of her courage.

Lucie raised three children while going through trauma after trauma and she made sure every lesson she learned was passed on to those children. Amazing. The determination was something to behold, a fight that I certainly would not have been able to put up. She did and she's here today publishing her first book. The adventure continues Lucie . . .

With Love,
Gordon

Introduction

I ADMIT IT. I WAS SOMEWHAT ÓF A DRAMATIC child. But somewhere between the drama and the actual childhood traumas, a space within me opened up and I gave it permission to exist. I allowed it in without ever knowing I had a choice. It began to take over and rule my life. I was no longer a dramatic child, but an anxious child. Unfortunately, I was the only one that knew the difference. And therein began the extremely painful, yet eventful (and sometimes even funny) journey of Lucie versus Anxiety.

I would love to say this book ends beautifully. That I learn all the lessons and follow them like a good grasshopper, becoming wise beyond my years. That I catapult myself into the stratosphere of healing gurus, waving my magic wand at others and help them destroy the anxiety monster that they too have done battle with and want so badly to release.

Nope. Not even close. This is not that book.

Although I would absolutely love a magic wand. And a thin waistline, but I digress.

But please read on, because I think we are more alike than we are different.

I do believe that there is a common thread that

weaves us all together, and it is that connection that creates the curiosity to want to know the story and cheer when there is triumph over adversity. It may not be your story, but mine is just different in the details. I am happy to take you on this cerebral journey about how anxiety can spiral out of control and how I learned to enjoy the ride.

Part 1

taking it in

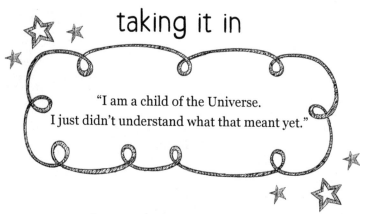

"I am a child of the Universe.
I just didn't understand what that meant yet."

I once asked a very wise man.
while in the depths of anxiety suffering
"What are the worst anxiety symptoms?"
He paused. Then simply said.
"Yours."
No truer words were ever spoken.

1
And The Award
Goes To . . .

"I would like to accept this award on behalf of me.
I am the keeper and the releaser (is that a word?)
of what resides within.
I choose to let go of what doesn't serve me
and focus on the potential that rests inside
just waiting to be woken.
But not just yet.
I have shit to learn first."

"LUCIE YOU ARE SO DRAMATIC."

"Lucie you are going to win an Academy Award one day with that crying."

"Just stop it. You are way too sensitive."

^ Words I heard growing up.

I wanted so badly to be the perfect kid. The fifth of six kids, I really did want attention. I craved it. I thought perfect would be the way to cast the spotlight on me and away from everyone else. But if I was being told I was too sensitive, obviously there was something wrong with me. I needed to fix that, but the more I tried, the more entangled I was with what came to be known as me being a drama queen.

There were other words that I heard growing up, such as:

"You are so smart."

"You are beautiful."

"What a great singer you are."

As a kid who wanted to be perfect, I did not focus on what sounded great. I could have gotten compliments and high praises for weeks straight, but it would be the one . . .

"You are too sensitive."

. . . that would get stuck in my head. The words that I deemed negative were the ones I focused on, and I tried to figure a way out. To be the opposite of. To pull the sensitivity out of my body and replace it with a stoic warrior.

The more I tried, the more sensitive I became.

I believed the hype.

I believed what I was told.

Words were everything to me.

And I let them seep into my subconscious that was working hard to create my life's foundation.

My belief system.

I am sensitive.

I overreact.

#deal

2
Soap Tastes Awful

"There are three sides to every story.
Your side. My side.
And the one that will not get me in trouble."

WE WERE ALL LINED UP. I WAS FOUR, WHICH means my sisters that were part of this debacle were teenagers. He said there was someone who did something very bad in the house. I knew what it was. Guilt was invading my being as he spoke. But I didn't want to admit to the crime. I was going to lie.

"Someone left this purse on the floor with everything spilled out and gum wrappers by the garbage. Who did it?" By his glare in my direction I knew maybe I didn't fool this man, my father.

I quickly swallowed the gum.

He was holding the purse cupped in his hands, still unzipped, like it was the Holy Grail.

He went down the line of children, one at a time, asking in a calm but very scary voice:

"Did you go in your mother's purse without permission?"

Each sister responded the same, a quiet no with a shake of their head. When he got to me, I too mimicked my role models with the same nod. However, my nod seemed to be dismissed. And rather quickly I was tried and sentenced. He told the sister closest to me in proximity to wash my mouth out with soap for lying.

She escorted me to the bathroom. As she stuck the bar in my mouth, she whispered in a sweet sisterly voice:

"Don't bite down on it and don't let it touch your tongue."

When it was over, she lovingly helped me get a cup to gargle my way out of the nasty taste. I was ashamed that I lied, and even more so that I had soap in my mouth. I internalized it and created the belief that I was a liar. Yes, I lied. I get it. But I did not have to wear it as a badge. But I did. Because I was a drama queen you see . . .

And it was about this age that I began assigning labels to myself. These labels became how I identified myself and how I chose to see the world.

It was a few years later that I found myself at my desk in first grade feeling very hot.

I was scared to raise my hand. I knew I was sick, but I wasn't sure that I would be believed. You see I was a liar. The great gum liar. And because of that I did not want anyone to even think I was lying, even if

I was telling the truth. I didn't want to get in trouble. Remember I am a perfectionist in training, that over-reacts and now is a liar. It's a lot to keep straight for a six-year-old.

Finally getting the courage to raise my hand, I flung it high for her to see.

"Yes, Lucie?"

"I feel hot. Can I go to the nurse?"

"Put your head down for a few minutes," she said ever so sweetly. (I loved this teacher. Putting your head down on a desk was a common way back then to take a small break and evaluate if you really were not feeling well.)

See. She didn't believe me I thought. I put my head down and every part of my being was screaming I need help, but I dare not move. I didn't want to overreact or be called a liar. I wanted to be perfect. She would have never called me anything, she was wonderful, but I was scared. Just in case she did think I was faking, I didn't want to call any more attention to myself. I collected myself, put my head back up and forced a smile on my very hot face.

When school was over, I began my trek home. Within the first few minutes I remember feeling quite dizzy, then I fainted right on the school sidewalk. When I came to, I saw my teacher running towards me. She scooped me up and brought me home. My parents thanked her and took me to the hospital where I was admitted for some time with double pneumonia.

Sitting under that tent in the hospital, all alone at night, gave me ample thinking time. I began ruminating. Going over again and again what I could have done differently. What I could have done to be believed or less dramatic.

I mean the whole kit and kaboodle was ridiculously dramatic:

- me walking home and fainting.
- my teacher finding her dying student on the side of the road.
- me placed in a tent in a special room in the hospital.

I am certain my family was crazy concerned. That was not the story I told myself though. I beat myself up inside. You are overreacting again. Look at you in this tent. This happens to no one else I know. It is because you are wrong and need fixing. You are not perfect.

Breathing in the plastic night after night in the hospital room, I thought maybe this is where I belong. Where people who are not perfect get help.

Soap – 1

Lucie – 0

#gameon

3
Playing House

"Being a child is dangerous.
There is something that can hurt you
even in the most innocent of games."

I WAS LIGHT YEARS AHEAD OF THE LAUNDRY pod challenge. Except I ate dishwashing detergent. And it was blue crystals, not a pod. I chugged the chemicals from the aluminum spout on the side of the box.

I was pretending we were having dinner. I was very young. We were playing house. I love food.

Immediately I felt fire on my gums.

The roof of my mouth.

My cheeks.

Instinctively I began spitting. But somehow that made it feel worse.

I cannot remember what my brother was doing during this or who called the ambulance.

There had to have been an adult home? Probably one of my sisters called.

The ambulance shows up. I'm dying. Right? Ambulance clearly means I am on the brink of death. I was handed something they said would taste like lemonade and instructed to drink it all.

It tasted gross. I think I threw up.

And when I came home it was never mentioned.

I must just be someone who does weird things and gets sick.

Is that who I am?

#iamweird

#lifeisdangerous

4
Crank Up The Tunes

"I went into the woods thinking camp rocks.
I came out of the woods knowing I would never go
back in the woods."

HE SAID HE WANTED TO GET ME BEFORE I WAS older and hot. At least I think those were his words, if not exact pretty damn close. He was the assistant counselor in charge of me and a few other kids for our end of camp sleepover. We walked the trail to find a spot to put our sleeping bags. He was walking behind me and I remember he touched my hip and I grabbed his hand to pull it away. Somehow his shorts ripped a little on a branch. He told me that was me being frisky.

I didn't understand any of his words. I was 11.

That night he touched me.

I woke with a nauseous stomach. My mind racing that I did something very wrong and that I would never be able to show my face anywhere again. Who lets

someone touch them? Especially a high school boy. Do other people touch each other? Or am I tainted for life?

We made our way out of the woods and back to the camp headquarters, I cried as he proudly announced to everyone what happened between us. He was laughing and running around with a bunch of boys and pointing at me. There was an older counselor that noticed me crying and she came over to talk with me. I told her I was so embarrassed and she said don't worry about it that it will blow over.

Her boom box was sitting on the picnic table blaring Cheap Trick. All I could hear was, "I want you to want me. I need you to need me. I love you to love me . . ." I began to shake and this fear came over me that was somewhat familiar at this point, but seemed so much more than it ever had. I turned up the music because I couldn't think of anything else to do as I watched him—this horrible boy—laughing and looking over at me. My stomach was churning and I started shaking uncontrollably. The music was drowning the fear just a little. Something broke inside of me at that moment.

I went back to school that fall and told a couple friends. They were horrified. In fact, one of them told me I was lying. I am a liar—the great gum liar—but this was true. And now I am not just a liar, but horrifying because I was touched. What is wrong with me?

I began to isolate myself after this. I would lock myself in the laundry room and sit on the floor with all the laundry. It is where I belonged, on the floor breathing in all the bleach and detergent fumes. This is where I would cry and ask God for help.

#thewoodsaredangerous

#iambroken

#laundrysmells

#nooneknew

5
Don't Pass Notes in School, Dear . . .

"Some lessons you learn are so misguided
and they shape your everything."

I KNEW AS SOON AS I PASSED THE NOTE, SHE
had me. She was good. Eyes like a hawk, always searching. My teacher eyeballed me as she snatched the note
out of my friend's hand.

"Lucie, we will talk after class."

Me sinking in my seat.

I watched the large round clock on the wall as the
seconds ticked by, following the movement of the out
of sync long skinny hand. Forever was an understatement.

As kids finally shuffled out, I stayed.

"Do you understand how cruel this note is?"

"Yes."

"Do you have anything to say?"

"I am sorry." I really wanted to say what she was

talking about was way over my head but I didn't. I still didn't understand love. Or sex. And after the *camp in the woods* incident I wanted to understand, but my mind was on guard about it. Nothing about sex seemed safe, it just made me scared. And so, instead, I wrote about it and made fun of it. Her talking about sex. My note just said that she was boring us with all her talk about sex.

Oh, and that other thing I wrote.

"I will not give this note to the other teacher you wrote about. I know you are sorry."

"Thank you. And yes I am."

Flash forward two hours later and I settle in for my afternoon class. I notice this teacher has the note I wrote about her gripped in her fingers. I was stunned because my morning teacher had said she was not going to hand it over. I knew immediately I was toast.

"Lucie, out in the hallway, now!"

I got up from my desk and proceeded out the door. As I slowly walked my walk of shame, I heard the simultaneous "ohhhhhhhh . . ." of my peers. This outburst was the common utterance that had come to mean *you are in trouble*.

Once out in the hallway, she began immediately screaming at me. Let me rephrase that: she was frothing at the mouth, while simultaneously grinding her teeth and spitting as she yelled at me. Then it got really scary . . . she got quiet and just stared at me. Her gaze into my little girl soul hurt, but I stood my ground and looked back. I recall *feeling* a fear in my teacher that I could not understand. Obviously being young, I had no idea about life wounds and triggers. My note had provoked something in her that hurt her beyond comprehension. I felt bad. I was responsible for this hurt and I wanted to make it better.

Breaking the silence, my teacher whispered something inaudible. Then she stopped and looked at me with her eyes welled up to the point of overflow. I assumed this was now my turn to respond.

"I am sorry." Damn, was I. I wasn't sure what to do here. I was scared. She was right to be mad. I was wrong.

"If you do not get a 100% on the test tomorrow, I am going to call your parents and tell them about this note. Understand?"

Definitely not what I was expecting. My mind began racing about how much trouble I would get into if my parents got a call. This was in the days that no matter what, if your parents got a call from your teacher, you were wrong.

"Okay." This was the only thing I could think to say. I did not want to add to her terrifying anger. Her tear streaked skin was apparent as we both entered the classroom again. Kids were silent as if they could read the energy of what just happened. The rest of the class was silent study for the upcoming test. I felt terrible that I hurt my teacher.

You better believe I knew every freaking answer on the test that day. I had to be perfect.

Perfect takes away the hurt. Perfect makes people happy. Perfect gets me out of trouble.

#nophonecall
#perfectionrocks
#nomorenotes
#startedadiary
#writingrocks

6
School Is For Learning

"Learning comes in so many forms."

I WALKED TO OUR LOCKERS AS I DID EVERY morning.

"Good Morning!" I said bouncing around still excited from the night before.

The night before was everything to me. I was part of a show where I got to sing.

I was in the spotlight. I loved being up on stage. I felt alive doing what I loved.

"Hey, guys, good morning?"

Nothing. Heads turned.

My mind raced. What did I do? Why are they not talking to me?

This must be a joke. That's it. A joke.

But no one was laughing. They shut their lockers and walked away.

. . . come back, please, you are my people.

That day was hard.

None of them spoke to me.

I had to escape. I went to the nurse and somehow, I had a fever.

I was sick. A sick that I could not describe.

I went home and was scared to go back the next day.

And the next day. And the day after that.

They didn't want to be my friend any more

I came back to school.

School was scary now.

I maneuvered quickly from classroom to classroom so I would not have to see them.

I sat alone at lunch. I am sure I could have sat with others.

I had friends from my neighborhood, they probably would sit with me.

But I didn't want to attempt it. I didn't want to take the chance and be rejected.

That hurt too much. I don't want to feel that ever again.

I didn't do anything. What's wrong with me?

I quickly formed some thoughts in my head.

It's not safe to shine.

Something is wrong with me.

^ The stories I told myself stuck.

I hid within them.

#hidinginmystory

7
Family And Food
Perfect Together

"Coping skills are the keys.
I just do not know yet what they open."

MY MOM WAS A FANTASTIC COOK. SO WAS MY nana. And so many other relatives. We grew up on good, homemade food. Italian food. One of my earliest memories is of me standing on a chair, flush against the counter, on tippy toes. There was an assembly line of working relatives to the left of me, doing their part to construct the ravioli. When this beautiful piece of filled dough reached me, it was my job to seal the two pieces together with the tines of the fork. The deeper the marks the better the seal.

The smell of homemade sauce on the back burner would waft through the kitchen as the voices of women, one louder than the other, would be music to my ears. I learned laughing was what *we* did. It was the way we dealt with things. No matter the conversation,

I noticed that they ended with a cackling laugh. I adopted that. I needed laughter.

In the dining room were the men. They were talking and laughing as well. I could hear the roar building as one told the other something funny and contagiously the laughter built to a crescendo and then slowly petered out. This repeated many times over. My little ears waited for the chorus of sounds that put a smile on my face through the wall that separated the kitchen from the dining room.

Holidays. Summer picnics. Special events. My house. We were that home. I always had aunts, uncles and cousins over. It was the norm. Even among all the people, though, I felt alone. Actually, I did not feel alone, I felt lonely if that makes any sense at all. Among all the relatives, I somehow felt distant and I learned that it was the laughter that helped me hang on. Hearing a note of levity in my heavy heart would give me the belief laughter could make it all okay.

"Lucie, you okay?"

"Of course." I would say with a chuckle.

The chuckle was code to everyone (it seemed) that all was good.

#copingskills
#foodandlaughter
#itwasntallgood

8
Baked Ziti

"Please don't assume that you think like I do.
Everyone experiences loss differently."

MY FRIEND'S FAMILY BROUGHT BAKED ZITI. IT was such an incredible gesture. She sat with me and hugged me, my friend. I needed that. I was happy to have someone come over and talk with me, because I felt more alone than ever. Everyone is wearing black. Crying. Laughing. Hugs. Large amounts of food.

I went to school the following Monday. I heard the whispers.

"I can't believe she is here."

"She must not have loved her father."

It hurt. These comments were meant for me to hear, but thankfully most people were not this cruel. Mostly the kids in school just ignored it. Or didn't care. Or didn't know. While at school it seemed like it never happened. My father's death. I was 14. It was sudden and awful. I wanted to be at school. I needed

the structure and the normalcy. I had loss. I felt loss.
I was lost.

There was no one to speak with at the school, aside
from the guidance department. And I thought maybe
they were more about the college application process,
not the human is hurting process. I didn't know. Coun-
seling was not really "a thing" back then, or if it was, I
was not aware of how to go about such services. To be
honest, I had no idea I needed help. No one at home
was speaking about it. No one at school was talking to
me. Okay, I thought. This is how we deal with death.
With trauma. We just push it down.

I had no one to speak with.

Back to the laundry room. Lock the door. Cry.

Come out clean, just like the laundry.

Happy face. Sad soul. Trudge on.

#ilovebakedziti

#grief

#foodanddeath

#noonetalks

#keepitin

9
Let The Sun Shine

"It cannot be described.
The neighborhood was everything.
It was the fun. The laughter. The safe zone."

EVERY DAY WAS A DIFFERENT ADVENTURE. I would come home, open the garage door with the automatic opener that was hidden in the grille. I would let myself in and grab a snack. Homework quick, then out I went. I had the neighborhood.

All that was needed was to begin walking down the street. Within seconds you were met by others and soon your daily squad was formed. There was no discrimination or cliques. Maybe there were, but my child self didn't notice. I just wanted to be part of it all.

Doors were open, parents waving. Bikes, skateboards or your own two feet got you from one place to another. It didn't matter. It was all good. Sometimes we just sat and talked, other times we used our imagination and put on plays. As I grew up, the neighborhood became more important. I needed the community for my own sanity. I would walk to the creek or ride my moped to look for shark teeth and frogs. There were always kids to hang out and share your afternoons with. Outdoors was a must. It was part and parcel to being a kid.

We would stay out until dark. And then we would scramble in all directions to get home just on time. Every parent had a different call for their child. A bell, a whistle, a scream. And each kid knew if they were called more than once, they were late. Washing up was a must because we were dirty. Or at least I was. I lived for nature, for friends and for the adventure. Dinner would be every night at the table, with the family.

It was structure. It was safe. It was community.

My mom went back to work after my dad died. Dinners were no longer at the table. She worked and came home, tired. I learned to use the microwave pretty well and *cooked* for me and my brother. I began to hide from the community. I had friends, but I would retreat often. I had no words for it. I thought I was being anti-social or mean. Who knew what depression and anxiety was in those days? I sure didn't. I craved fun, but just couldn't create it anymore.

I could not understand my actions and attitude. A perfect, gum lying, sickly-scared, touch-tainted, grief-stricken kid just keeping it real. I felt like stuff was welling up inside and getting to be too much.

#stopoverreacting

#gettingfull

10
How About Some Sugar, Sugar?

"What diet?"

MY MOM WAS NOW WORKING. A LOT. SHE HAD to. She had to keep a house over our heads. She not only worked a full-time day job, she worked nights cleaning. There was a huge shift in our family dynamic. There were no more large gatherings of Italian Sunday Dinners. There were not any more morning breakfasts or packed lunches. A sit-down dinner was a rarity. We all had to pitch in and make this work. I learned to grow up really fast after my father's death, but I honestly had no idea what I was doing. And I had that pesky thing that kept happening making me feel weird in my body, the shaking and the fear. I just ignored it.

My mom did a great job of keeping her stress hidden. She showed really no emotions about anything. Of course, I know now she was being strong for us, but back then I just assumed that showing feelings was a weakness and even more so, an indicator that something was wrong.

I didn't want to add to her load and have her worry about me and meals. So, I began eating whatever I wanted. It was liberating. No veggies. No protein. Just what I chose.

My lunch in high school. Every. Single. Day.

- bagel
- candy bar
- soda

Not sure whether to bless or curse the 1980's for my ability to eat this and call it a healthy lunch. Dinner was normally a deli sandwich with a candy bar and soda. Snack at night was candy. Pre-packaged cupcakes and chocolate rolls with cream filling were the staples in my diet.

It was during this time I recognized my sugar addiction. Although, it was not called an addiction back then, it was a "give Lucie a candy bar, she is getting angry" discussion. I ate like this morning, noon and night. Vegetable was a bad word. And water? Who drank water?

Iced Tea. Tang. Soda. The holy trinity of liquids.

It didn't seem to bother me though. I stayed a steady weight and felt healthy.

Friends remarked how they could not understand how I could eat the way I did and not gain a pound. I just did. I considered myself lucky.

Of course, I wasn't lucky.

I just didn't know it yet.
#ishouldhavehadaV8

11
The Reaction

"I have a problem.
I don't want to be different."

I WAS AN AMAZING STUDENT IN GRADE school.

Like off the charts smart.

Now I was anything but.

I no longer tried. Or cared.

Maybe I cared but just didn't know how to change back to the old happy Lucie.

I did not like the person I saw when I looked in the mirror.

I left school one day, right smack in the middle of the day to smoke a joint with some friends.

We were standing in my friend's garage and passing it around talking and laughing about a lot of nothing.

Everyone else seemed fine, but I was feeling really strange.

I felt paranoid. But also, like I was in extreme danger.

We got back to school and I was feeling even more odd.

"Hey, you guys feel okay?" I asked hoping they were feeling the way I was.

"Yeah, I feel great."

"Sooooo great," said another laughing.

I began to hallucinate. I *saw* a mouth on the backside of my neck and it was talking. Yep, that is what happened right in the middle of our locker pit. I was so freaked out; I began running around and saying things in a really weird garbled voice. Someone handed me water in a cup and when I took a sip it felt like I was drinking sand. It weighed me down. I was so thirsty, but did not want any more sand, so I went outside and began eating the snow off the ground.

And in case you are wondering, yes there was snow on the ground. That part was not a hallucination.

I was so hot and thirsty, I actually not only ate the snow, but dropped down and rolled in it to try to cool off. One of the guys said I should go home—so I did.

I got into my 280zx and turned up the tunes on my removable radio.

"Life in the Fastlane" was playing and I found that extremely ironic in my current state.

In no way should I have been driving, but I made it home.

I remember lying on my bed and closing my eyes and all I kept seeing was my skeleton and flashing lights. My mom got home from work and I told her I think I need to go to the emergency room. She was so concerned and was adamant I tell her where I got the pot from. I didn't tell. Heck, I couldn't remember. All I kept saying to her was, "I am going to die." And she held me and said I was not going to die and to calm down. I was happy for her comfort, but I truly thought I was going to die.

However, under my fear was an inner voice mocking me: "You are overreacting again. No one else reacted like this. Of course, you are. This is how it goes for you." These were always the words that went around in my head.

#notnormal

#ioverreact

#thingsworkdifferentforme

12
Love?

"I had no boundaries. It was open season."

THERE WAS ONE THAT WOULD SQUEEZE MY arm until it would bruise.

And another that would scream at me just for sport.

One that was jealous and didn't let me talk with friends.

Or the one that ignored me and put more effort into his drug habit than our relationship.

Why did no one see?

Why didn't I see?

I never told anyone. I was ashamed of myself.

I seemed to have it together on the outside.

I didn't want to admit that I allowed these intrusions upon body and mind

. . . and even more so, my soul.

I continued the pattern of terrible choices in boyfriends.

The abuse. The pain. I just let it happen. I let it unfold.

What boundaries?

What was going on inside of me that allowed such horrible respect for myself? I wasn't sure.

I saw my friends with their boyfriends and they were always laughing and having such a great time. I craved this relationship. I didn't know how to get it. To attract it.

I must deserve this.

I am so broken.

#gavemypoweraway

#unworthy

13
What's That Smell?

"When others hear sirens,
I want to tell them that is what it is like
to be in my head 24/7."

WE WERE JUST LEAVING MAMMA MIA PIZZA (was that the name of the place?) and getting in my car when I heard the sirens. My friend and I were laughing, but she didn't notice I was looking around because I am always scanning.

Alert.

Looked above and saw the smoke.

"Wow, that fire must be close. Let's follow that fire engine!"

High Alert.

We follow it and it stops at my house.

Of fucking course it's my house.

My heart is beating so fast. No time for tears.

Is everyone okay? Who was home?

I have to make sure all is okay. That is my job. Making it all okay.

Brother home. He is okay. Thank God.

The fire is out. One room gone. Smoke damage to rest of the house.

Did we ever talk about it?

I don't talk about it. No one does.

Alert is over. Silenced? Never.

Keep scanning Lucie. It is your job to scan for emergencies.

Is this overreacting?

#thisiswhyioverreact

#becauseshitdoeshappentome

#ineedtoremainvigilant

14
Come Home from the Party Please

"There are no words for grief.
Even the word grief itself seems a bit insulting
by trying to encapsulate the enormity
of it into one word."

IT WAS SUMMERTIME. JUST LEFT COLLEGE with amazing grades and a new attitude.

I was happy to be home with my high school friends.

It was a beautiful summer night, with just the right amount of coolness in the air. I was wearing white pants that came below my knee, a double pair of wigwam socks, also white, and Candie's sneakers, that were, you guessed it, white. On top I had a green Guess sweatshirt cardigan, a bit oversized, as was the fashion, which was the perfect backdrop to my long-permed hair. I felt like a million bucks this particular night. I was with my best friends at a party. To be honest, I have no memory of which friend's house it was, but we were happy enough milling about with our red solo cups filled to the rim from the keg outside.

There were a group of boys on top of a car with a boom box, blasting Guns n Roses "Sweet Child of Mine." It seemed as though the entire party was singing along to this fantastic song that just epitomized the summer, being young and having fun. I was laughing and smiling, and I remember thinking at one point this is one of the best nights of my life. My thoughts were abruptly interrupted

"Your mom is looking for you, she wants you home now."

"What, who did she call?"

"Apparently she has been calling everywhere looking for you."

So weird. I finish my beer and ask my friend for a ride home.

We have the radio blasting to Van Halen (the Sammy days) on the way home, singing at the top of our lungs. As she pulls into the driveway, I am giggling, thinking I must be in trouble for something. I tell my friend I will call her later. I shut the car door and begin my staggered walk into the house.

I proceed up the stairs, but even before I could look them, I felt the energy in the house. It was a familiar feeling, as I had heard news like this before. Five years earlier to be exact, when I received the news about my father's death. I wanted to run, but there was no escaping from what was about to unfold. I looked up and my eyes captured the scene in one take. I remember someone saying to me, "You look beautiful."

They were talking, but I was not listening. I didn't need to hear it all, got the key words. Sister. Dead. Sudden. Drugs.

I slowly made my way down the hallway and closed my bedroom door. So many random and odd thoughts were running through my brain. How could a night that seemed so perfect end with this? Why was my sister so sad? Why didn't I see the signs? What did it feel like to die? Why would she do this to herself? To us? What does this mean? What happens next?

I ignored the knocking at my door and called a friend.

The next week was filled with the hustle and bustle of death. Familiar and horrific. Just beginning to understand this thing we called adulthood, I was confused by the entire process. There was crying, laughing and lots of eating. I would retreat often to my room to try to make sense of it all. Of everything. Not just of her death, but of life, of purpose and of the universe and its enormity.

#sosad
#badthingshappenaftergoodtimes
#loveeveryone
#peopleleave
#survivorguilt

15
If This Is Help,
No Thank You

"When you tell your story,
make sure you add laughter.
Because crying just ruins your makeup."

I MADE IT BACK TO COLLEGE.

How? Not so sure. But I am thriving. More than thriving.

Blossoming. I am making friends and learning by watching others how a non-overreactor behaves. I try on their mannerisms and mimic their attitude.

I begin to write. It's my therapy.

It reminds me of when I wrote in my diary every day when I was younger. I write for a teacher who encourages more writing. She is my angel.

"Lucie, your writing is excellent and the stories are beautiful. Can we agree to create an independent study class for you so you can obtain credit for writing short stories?"

"Can we do that? Yes, of course. I would love that. Thank you." Someone is *allowing me* to express my feelings and put them down on paper. This is amazing. As it begins to pour out, I am not sure I can handle everything that is being written.

I am carrying so. much. grief.

I go to a counselor, who begins crying when my story unfolds.

She looks a wreck, sitting there with streams of tears down her cheeks.

It is hard for me to process this. The very person I thought could help me is a mess and I am consoling her. I assume now that *everything* is on my back. All the responsibility of my family. All the responsibility of death and grief. And now the responsibility of other people and their feelings. I need to be guarded so not to make someone upset.

It's too much.

I am not going back to her.

She calls constantly to check on me on my phone in my dorm room.

I ignore her calls.

I cannot be responsible for the happiness of the person who is supposed to help me.

Frick. My counselor is an overreactor too.

#mytribe?

#sensitive

#overreactors

#myjob

16
Really Where Is
The Italian Food?

*"I need to be in control, said everyone
at some time point in their life."*

THERE WAS A NEW PHENOMENON SWEEPING
college campuses called frozen yogurt.

I heard girls talking about how they could limit
food and be skinny. That yogurt could be a meal and
make you full without many calories.

I was hooked. It was my dinner every night without fail. A frozen chocolate yogurt with carob chips.
The weight started coming off. This was interesting I
thought. I could do something—my actions had a di-
rect result—I decided to go further . . .

a handful of cereal
plain chicken baked
a handful of cereal
frozen yogurt with carob chips

That four-item list was my new diet in college. A

full day consisted of just cereal, some chicken and yo-gurt. Every now and again I would have a bagel, but that was rare.

I had control. If the diet varied any reason one day, I would be more aware the next day. I counted every calorie.

I didn't know what anorexia was. I kind of did, but not really. I certainly did not have it; I was just shed-ding the extra weight I had put on. Right?

Screw everyone that told me I had to eat more. I looked great; they were just jelly.

I still laughed. I still went out.

There was just a lot less Lucie to hang out with.

Was this on purpose? Was I pulling a disappearing act?

No. I was in freaking control. Nothing more was going to happen in my life.

I am in control.

Fuck food.

I don't need no stinkin' food.

#ofcourseitwasanorexia

#ihadtocontrolsomething

#foodwasalwaysacopingtool

#reversecoping?

17
There Is Always Laughter

"Sometimes you have to laugh so hard you pee.
Sometimes you probably should just laugh.
Skip the pee."

I JUST LIT UP A MARLBORO LIGHT.

My friends came running out of the store into the mall. They stampeded down the stairs by JC Penny. They were gone in a flash. Trying to keep their pace, I follow them.

Somewhere after a bunch of steps, I trip. It is important to note as I trip going down, there is a woman who appears to be in her mid-thirties, shopping bags in hands, climbing up the stairs.

I begin to fall from my clumsy mishap and I collide into this woman.

Unfortunately, we become entangled and together we fall downward one step at a time, rolling and screaming. My Marlboro Light plays a heavy role in this story. You see, as we were coupled together my cigarette burns her, multiple times. I know this because she repeats "ow!" every time it makes contact with her arm. I feel awful, as I can't stop the madness, and we continue our descent.

Finally, we land off the stairs onto the mall floor. Oddly enough, our position in landing was me straddling her. Her pinned to the floor.

We are face to face.

Emotions filled me, including laughter, as I could not believe what just happened. As I looked into this poor woman's eyes, sitting on top of her and giggling uncontrollably, I peed on her. Literally. Must have been a combo of fear, humor and shock, but yes, I peed on her.

And then I got up and ran.

I preferred this Lucie. The one that laughed so hard she peed. It made me forget all the other stuff.

I know karma is a bitch.

To date I have not been peed on.

Or have I?

#islifejustabigpissparty?

#uselaughterlucie

#coping

18
Home. Less.

*"I had yet to understand that the home
I was looking for was already inside of me.
However, I really would have loved a bedroom."*
Lucie

WE WENT FROM THE HOUSE I GREW UP IN . . .
to a condo . . . to my mom renting a one-bedroom
apartment. Mostly happening all while I was in college. The family bankruptcy was just another reminder to me that life is full of fear and disappointment. I
felt awful that I was not there to help my mom, but
I knew that getting an education was what I needed
to do in order to make money and contribute in some
way.

When I could no longer be out of state to go to college because of the cost, I stayed home and commuted
to college. With all the transfers, I still graduated in
four years, because I knew I had to. There was no extra
money and I already had a loan that needed to be paid.

I graduated with a degree in English and went

right to work, not as a writer like I wanted, but at the local mall. I needed to work no matter the job.

At this point I was helping my mom in any way I could. But I needed to get an apartment. I could not sleep on the couch. My younger brother needed to sleep there and I could only sleep in the bathtub so many times! (Two reasons I was in the bathtub—the only space to sleep and because even if I could find room to park myself around the apartment, the snoring from nameless family members was way too loud!)

This is when miracles started happening. Or maybe they were happening my entire life because being born while your mother was on the pill is sort of a miracle, but I was just now noticing.

I got a message from this man that said he viewed my resume and would like me to come in for an interview at his company. I never sent my resume out. It was a miracle how it ended up in his hands. This turned into a job—no it turned into a career. I was able to move out. To get an apartment. To help my mom. And that is not all the universe had planned for me. There was much more to come.

I thought this was the end of overreacting. Of being dramatic. Of shit.

Not so, but it was a beginning. I like beginnings.

#newstart?

#suckitsoap

#canibegintobelieveingood

19
Love Does Exist

"Sometimes it takes someone else to believe in you before you can see it."

HE ASKED ME OUT A BUNCH OF TIMES.

We worked together and I thought he was cute . . .

I turned him down every time.

I felt like I did not deserve him.

He did not give up, thankfully.

He told me he saw something in me that he wished I could see for myself. He was in a band. One night at a party he dedicated a song to "the beautiful girl in the audience."

He began singing while playing the guitar.

He locked onto my eyes the entire song.

Words like "beautiful . . . and just don't realize . . . and eyes . . . how much I love you . . ." were directed towards me. I was speechless. And scared. Terrified more like it.

He was different.

The moment we began dating I told him all the good, the bad and the ugly that I was carrying around with me. He smiled. It was okay. It was all okay he said. And he meant it.

This man became my husband.

It was the beginning of a beautiful union.

It was also the point when I started to believe a little more in myself.

Boy was I going to need it, that belief. Why?

Because all that I bottled up from childhood would eventually need to come out.

I know I told my husband about everything,

but if I could have seen into the future, I would have told him to buckle up and get ready

—and to wear a helmet,

because we were going to experience one heck of a ride together.

#thingswerelookinggood

#foundmysoulmate

Part 2

Going Within

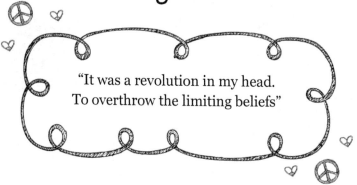

"It was a revolution in my head.
To overthrow the limiting beliefs"

I once asked myself
"How did I get here?"
And how can I get out of this suffering?"
I thought, then simply said,
"Me."
Just this one-word was everything to be spoken.

20
My Baby And Me

"I Didn't Expect This When Expecting."

"YOU ARE GOING TO NEED A C-SECTION."

"What are you talking about?" I didn't read the fucking section in the book about c-sections, I read the chapter about breastfeeding my child while lounging in a gliding rocker, with a flowing white nightgown on. But honestly, after over twenty-four hours of labor; a couple hours of pushing, an epidural and an illegal amount of ice chips I was ready for whatever needed to be done. I wanted to meet my baby.

This. Is. Where. It. All. Changed.

All the crap that happened.

All the beliefs I formed.

All the shit I held in.

Came out.

There was a shift. And not one I was privy to.

I went into the hospital a smiling soon to be mom.

I left a freaking basket case. How? Read on.

As they lasered my belly, I made some wise ass comment that it smelled like burnt dog food. I recall the chuckles from the masked humans hovering above. If they were laughing and I continued to make them laugh, all was okay. But then—I heard a cry. His cry. It's a boy! The doctor lifted him up like Simba from the other side of the partition so that I could see. *My son is beautiful* is exactly what I was thinking. He was then brought next to me in an awkward position so it looked like his head was growing out of my shoulder. I couldn't move my arms, so I kind of pecked at him with my face. Not what I imagined. Pecking at my newborn as our first meeting. Then, someone snapped a picture which honestly seemed sinister. I mean how great could that picture be after having my insides taken out and then just five minutes later someone says, "Say cheese!" with a tiny head growing from my shoulder. Really? My son was then whisked away from me and I remember nothing more.

Hours later I groggily woke up in a strange room. Not a great start for someone with a short circuit in her alarm system. Immediately on alert, I looked around scouring for clues of my whereabouts. I felt like the Terminator, targeting my eyes to particular points in the room so I could assess the situation. Alert! Alert! The alarm went off. There was no baby.

"Where is my baby????" I tried to scream, but it came out a whisper. My husband was jolted awake from my quiet cry.

"He is in the nursery. I'll get him."

"No, don't."

Wait. What did I just say?

"Lucie, I'll get him. No worries, you don't have to move."

"No. Don't get him." I was disgusted by my words.

I went to cover my mouth as if I was teetering towards my third utterance of the forbidden word *Beetlejuice*. Why wouldn't I want my husband to get our baby for me to hold? I felt weird. No, I didn't feel weird. I couldn't feel weird because I didn't feel anything. I felt flat. Like Flat Stanley. Yes, Flat Stanley and I were compadres. We got each other. We had no dimensions. No feeling. We just went along for the ride. That was me right now.

Gordon ran to the nursery to get our son. I could tell he was concerned. So was I, but I tried to look unconcerned so not to make anyone feel uneasy. When Gordon came back into the room with our baby, I knew immediately I loved him, my son. I just couldn't feel it. Or feel love for my hubby. What was happening? I physically turned my back ever so slightly in my bed and away from the beautiful men in my life. My husband wasn't having it. He wheeled my son to the other side of the room and smiled a smile of concern. I gave him a head nod as if to say "all good." But I knew it wasn't all good. I knew I wasn't the same person; I just didn't understand why.

This was unchartered territory for me. I had been in many situations where shit had sucked. But I always felt, no matter what happened, I always felt *something*. Here I felt nothing. I was vacant. Flat Stanley. It was a little past midnight and I thought maybe this is all just from the surgery and concoction of drugs I was on. That it would all be fine in the morning.

It was then I noticed I was hooked up and connected to many different wires and tubes. By my side was something that resembled the Jeopardy answer button. Being who I am, I pushed it.

Feeling better.

A few minutes later I pushed it again.

Feeling even better.

I was like Pavlov's dog. I learned quickly this was a timed drug and as soon as I could get more, I would push the button and feel better.

Suddenly, I saw him. Bruce Vilanch. He just appeared in front of me, in center square. His hair wild and curious as always. He was telling a joke but I could not hear it very well, so I leaned forward in my bed to get within earshot of his voice. Gordon saw me laughing and talking to nothing. I explained matter-of-fact like that I was talking to Bruce from the game show Hollywood Squares. He summoned the nurse immediately. Not Bruce from Hollywood Squares, he didn't summon the nurse, that would be weird. My husband, he called the nurse. I was apparently having some amazing side effect to the morphine. I was hallucinating Bruce Vilanch. I really wanted my hubby and the nurse to stop their yapping because I missed the answer to the question which earned the contestant an X on Bruce Vilanch's square.

Needless to say, I was taken off the drip. Stat.

The next morning, I was determined to put everything from the night before away. Far. Far. Away. I wouldn't let myself think of it and when my baby was brought into my room I lovingly held him, kissed him and was happy to know I had some semblance of feelings going on.

My beautiful son and I bonded there, in that room for two nights. I held him. I fed him. We knew we had each other's backs for life. He was who made me a mommy. I loved him more than anything. During that stay it should have been just me and him getting to know one another, but there was a third visitor—a new visitor—I didn't have a name for it, but I felt its presence. It, whatever this *it* was, started to slowly (minute by minute) crowd out my joy.

When I was discharged, but my son was not, I was heartbroken. He had jaundice. I wanted to leave with my newborn, but instead I left empty-handed. I felt like a failure. And I was so pissed I left wearing my maternity clothes. That fucking book didn't tell me that either. Or maybe I just didn't read those parts . . . whatever. It sounds selfish that I was thinking about what I was wearing when the big thing was, I didn't have my son with me. But my mind was super scrambled and big things and little things all seemed to be equally important now. What was happening?

#justthebeginning
#strangerthingstocome
#overreactingforrealbegins

21
That Will Be
One Hundred Fifty Dollars

*"Sometimes the greatest thing
we can do for ourselves
is listen to what someone else is saying."*

IT WAS CHRISTMAS EVE 1999. I HAD A THREE-month-old baby and I had been on medication on and off for about a month now. I was told I had something called postpartum anxiety. I needed these drugs to work, but I was having crazy reactions to everything I tried. And the reactions were immediate. Large swollen arms. Red splotches everywhere. Psoriasis everywhere. Racing heart. Ginormous appetite. I thought sometimes maybe the anxiety would be better than the medication reactions, however I would have an episode and retract that thought! Drugs it is. Just needed to find the right ones.

It started slowly, the anxiety, but it quickly gained momentum. From the get-go I had only two speeds:

panic and flatness. I vacillated between anxiety and this weird sensation of not feeling like I was part of the world. I explained it to Gordon as if there was a divider up between me and everyone else, and I was not allowed to cross over into the rest of the world. I actually was more upset about these Flat Stanley sensations than the panic attacks. The anxiety consumed most every moment and never let up. Day or night. The brain I used to have was gone. It was replaced with a worry machine that thought irrationally and got me to react in the worst possible way to imagined emergencies. Not only was it scary, it was exhausting and consuming.

It all came to a head on Christmas Eve. It was my baby's first Christmas and I felt I should have been wrapping presents and cuddling up next to the fire with him. Although we did not have a fireplace, that is beside the point. It is my fantasy. And in it I am around a fireplace with my baby. Isn't that perfect and how it is supposed to be? Christmas music, fire and wrapping . . . right?

Instead I was in my bedroom, fetal position on the floor crying. I was on my fifth or sixth panic attack that day and I felt wiped out. This was a common occurrence, me crying on the floor after panic. Except this time there was a little twist. While I was sitting there an image popped in my brain. I imagined a scary monster-person running up my steps and killing me. Sounds silly, right? I thought so to, until the thought happened again. And again. And wouldn't stop. And it wasn't so much just a thought, but I could like feel the energy of someone or something running up my steps. I didn't see anything. I mean it was not the Bruce Vilanch hallucination again, but it felt real. I was super scared.

And then I heard something in my ear. Not something outside my ear, but inside, if that makes any sense at all. It was not a voice but more like an incredibly loud thought that flashed a *you are going to die* impression in my brain.

WTF?

I can't go crazy on Christmas Eve. Unacceptable. I am just overreacting I thought. But I wasn't. The stuff that was happening was real. I pulled out the yellow pages and started looking for a doctor. A psychiatrist. I needed to talk to someone and they need to straighten me out because I cannot lose my mind right now. It is Christmas. I have my family over and they are all downstairs while this is happening. You see, I am hosting Christmas Eve. Thank you very much. It is perfect downstairs, upstairs it is a shit show.

My husband begins calling the first person listed. Answering machine. Second one, machine. And so on. IT'S FREAKING CHRISTMAS EVE LUCIE. NO ONE IS GOING TO BE OPEN. But there is a monster-man in my head and I need help. Gordon keep calling. Please keep calling. And then it happens . . . he hands the phone to me.

"Hello?" I love and pity the person on the other end of the phone. Love her for answering. Pity her—like why are you in your office today woman?

"Hello, your husband says you need an emergency

meeting. If you can make it here within an hour, I will stay open."

Can I make it there in an hour? Does a bear shit in the woods? I mean I cannot believe we had the luck to find someone open. I begin pulling on boots and a sweater and I am actually smiling.

Someone is going to fix this mess. Yay! I run downstairs and explain very quickly that I will be back for Christmas Eve dinner, Gordon has the baby, I just need to pop out for a quick psych visit?????

Remember, my only experience with any type of talk therapy was one visit in college and the therapist cried, so my guard was up. However, I was also desperately hopeful for this visit to be the end of my panic. Running into her office out of breath, I make it there with five minutes to spare. I thought she would be annoyed, packed and ready to go. It was the exact opposite of my vision that I was met with. She was sitting in her chair, a cup of tea next to her looking incredibly relaxed. She smiled. I took my place across from her.

"Hello, Lucie."

"Hello, Doctor. Thank you for seeing me."

I regurgitated the last three months. She patiently listened.

At the end of the hour (really it is 45 minutes and what is that all about—the hour appointment that is actually 45 minutes?) she says:

"Lucie, you have really, really serious anxiety . . ." I think she mentioned lots of letters I didn't understand at the time like OCD and PTSD. "You need to go on medication," she said as she sternly looked through my eyes and into my soul.

"I am kind of scared of meds, with all the reactions and all."

"Take one here, so you feel safe if anything happens."

She gave me a script for an SSRI and then a script for a benzo drug.

The second one is the one I took in her office. And can I just say Hello Dolly! It was a magic pill. Within minutes I had no feelings of anxiety. All the hootin' and hollerin' in my head stopped. Just. Like. That.

I drove home with the music on, singing Christmas carols. But as I got closer to home, I began that feeling of being cut off from everyone else again. It was extreme, the flatness. I had no anxiety. I had no scary thoughts. I had nothing that bothered me. I just did not feel connected to anyone or anything all at the same time.

This doctor was a godsend for sure. She was my one-hundred-fifty-dollar weekly friend.

And I am not being facetious. She helped me see so much. But it was what I wasn't telling her that was the problem.

#keepingsecrets

#therewassomuchstillinside

22
What's Your Emergency?

*"It has been hard to keep it a secret.
But I didn't expect to announce it to the office
while being carted away."*

I HAD TWO MORE KIDS, SO NOW THREE. AND A
fabulous husband. And it wouldn't be a complete introduction to my family if I forgot to include anxiety.
In fact, anxiety had become a close second to my family in attention. Who am I kidding? Anxiety won. It always won my attention. It consumed my thoughts and
my life. Since that Christmas Eve over four years ago I
delicately walked the tightrope of hope. Unfortunately, I fell many times without a net to catch me. It was
when I was in these freefalls that I allowed anxiety to
grow and gain momentum.

After my third child I went on yet another medication. FYI the meds helped me. They really helped, *tem-
porarily*. They were a short-term solution for me and

well, unless you have been there please don't judge. With that being said, the new medication that I began taking created a Molotov cocktail inside my head.

I remember the night I took it. It was also the same night I went off a steroid drug. I was going to sleep that evening (after popping my pill) and when I closed my eyes, I saw flashing lights and colors. I also was simultaneously experiencing a panic attack. Peeps, a panic attack to me means extreme shaking, sweating, irrational thoughts, heart palps, pins and needles in my arms and legs, heat—lots of heat, vertigo and a number of other symptoms. It was not like, "Oh, I am a having a panic attack and I feel a little nervous." It was like, "I AM DYING A TERRIBLE, PAINFUL DEATH THAT I AM REQUIRED TO LIVE THROUGH."

Anyway . . . with all this going on, I tried to ignore it. Because that is what I was told to do. I could not understand how to ignore possible death, but okay. Ignore it is. I think I got maybe thirty minutes sleep that night, then went to work with my large iced coffee and bagel in hand.

Sitting at my desk, with a co-worker walking by, here is how this day went down:

"Morning."

"Morning."

"Blah blah blah (office banter)."

"More blah blah blah." I begin feeling weird.

He is talking to me, but he is blurry. Keep your shit together Lucie, no one knows how messed up you are. Ignore right? I get up from my seat, because I felt I needed to. Everything goes black and white. I am seeing everything in a blurry non-color way. Of course, my husband is off today. I want to run to him but he is home with the kids today. He would know what to do.

I stumble over to my friend at the front of the office. I whisper,

"Call 911—Call 911 something is going on."

She didn't bat an eye—or ask any questions—immediately she called. I fell to my knees and put my hands over my face and then rolled on my side. Somehow, miraculously I levitated into the other room. Of course, that is not what happened but I have no recollection of how I got from the front of the office to the back room, so in my story, I levitate (lol).

I was on the floor and couldn't handle anything. I was losing it. There were panic attacks, and warped feelings in my head that were indescribable. Danger alarms were sounding off everywhere in my body. I couldn't really speak, but I was crying and moaning. I remember lots of moaning. This is the part when it seemed like I was in a fishbowl. People formed a circle around me. I felt like a sideshow, but I was so scared I didn't care. They were saying things, but I could not decipher their words. All was in slow motion. I curled up in a ball and sobbed.

The ambulance came, finally. I heard people yelling about the fact that they were lost, so it was about 30 minutes before they got there. I was still in a ball as they picked me up and strapped me to the stretcher and wheeled me out of the office. A job I had for over fifteen years.

I remember being taken out of the ambulance and

seeing my husband and two kids standing there at the emergency room ambulance entrance. (The baby was with my mom). The look on my children's faces was terrifying. It was in that second. That exact fucking second when I saw their adorable little faces, I vowed to get myself out of this mess and make sure that I was the mom they needed so they could grow to be strong, confident, kind human beings that connected and plugged into life. I knew in that moment that even if anxiety was with me for the rest of my life, my focus was no longer going to be anxiety, it was going to be my family. My kids. I was breaking the cycle of crap, starting now.

Some may have called it a nervous breakdown. I called it my wake-up call. I would love to say this is where it got better, but there is some truth to the saying "it gets darkest before the light."

#bodytryingtotellme
#takearest
#whatisselfcare?

23
What I Planted, Grew

"This was the beginning.
The opening of a new world
that I had no idea existed."

ALTHOUGH I WENT BACK TO WORK AFTER THE nervous breakdown, things there were never the same.

Before I go any further, please let me remove any stigma of a nervous breakdown, because I sure as hell had judgements about that word. My nerves had enough, and broke down. Nothing more. Nervous breakdown. Easily defined.

My response to the incident was a learned pattern from childhood.

I didn't address it. I didn't talk about it.

I moved on. Went back to work the day after I got out of the hospital.

We needed the money.

I really longed to be home with my three children, but it was not an option.

The company was gracious and we worked out a part-time schedule.

The job that I loved for so many years changed. I had been a manager. I worked my way up the corporate ladder and was proud of my accomplishments. But now, part-time, I was given a cubicle in the corner of the office, doing work I despised.

For almost a year I would drag myself into work.

I ignored my body's attempt to get me out of a job that I no longer loved.

During this year my body became a stranger to me.

Panic attacks continued. I lost weight from the stress. Lots of weight. I was almost weightless.

I could no longer take any medication. Nothing. Reactions felt like assaults to my system.

It wasn't just the anxiety meds that I started to react to . . . I began reacting to the world.

Pesticides.

Perfumes.

Laundry Detergent.

Food.

Cleaning Products.

Plastics.

Makeup.

Any and all medications

I scoured the internet and one phrase kept coming up. MCS. Multiple Chemical Sensitivity. There were varying reasons why people got this condition. Some said it was an offshoot of anxiety. Other sites said it was a problem with the gut-brain connection and still others just said these were people with weakened systems. The pictures I saw frightened the shit out of me. I saw people living in motorhomes lined with tinfoil. People so very gaunt because they could not absorb any food. They lived in communes and away from others. This got my anxiety ramped up to a new level.

I did not want to live in a motorhome away from my family.

I went to a doctor; my first experience with an alternative doctor.

It was a far drive. There was a sign on the door "no perfume or scented soaps or deodorants please."

What world was I about to enter into?

"What can I do for you today Lucie?"

"Well, I know there are no scents allowed here, but I can smell the carpet, the table, your medical instruments. I am like a bloodhound."

"How does that make you feel?"

"Nervous. Scared. I want to run. But there is nowhere to go. Everywhere is a problem. There is nowhere safe."

After an exam and some more talking, I got the news that I already knew. I was diagnosed with MCS, alongside with the anxiety. Just peachy.

I couldn't hold back the tears as my husband watched. I knew he wanted to make it go away, but he didn't know how. This whole world was foreign to us.

As we were escorted to the front desk for treatment options, I peered into one of the rooms and saw multiple people hooked up to tubes sitting in seats. I asked and was told it was part of the healing protocol, massive amounts of Vitamin C and then other times Vitamin B12.

I was told I would probably be treating for months and then there is no guarantee it would work. It was all out of pocket. Thousands of dollars we didn't have.

I went home that night determined.

I slept with tinfoil under my sheets.

I mean, could it work?

Willing to try anything.

I wanted my food back.

Spoiler alert: No. Didn't work. For me.

#didntwork

#becamemyanthem

24
The Vampire

*"I knew it was all silly.
But this was how anxiety worked.
Nothing made sense."*

ANY LITTLE BLIP IN MY BODY WAS AN EMER-
gency. If my stomach hurt, I was dying. Possibly stomach cancer. If I had a headache it was a brain tumor. If
my foot hurt, I was needing an amputation. Any aches
and pains were amplified to the maximum. Anything
suspicious to me grew to outlandish proportions.

I needed to get a blood test. When you have anxiety, you tend to get lots of tests again and again. Just
for your own reassurance that nothing is wrong. I was
convinced I had a thyroid issue, even though the levels
were normal. There was a small school of thought that
said even in normal ranges if you feel your thyroid is
off, get further testing because it may uncover something more. So, I did.

Me being me, I had to go to the top guy. The specialist. I drove on back roads to the other side of the state to see him. His reviews were almost too good to be true. I had my Google Maps print-out of where his office was, and followed the directions perfectly. However, I could not believe this was the office of a famous doctor (famous meaning five-star internet reviews).

I walked in and there were some empty offices.

Did I mention this was a 7PM appointment?

No people. It was abandoned. I looked around and on a piece of yellow colored *construction paper* taped to the wall it said "Dr. _____ downstairs."

Basement. No one in building. Construction paper. Not a good feeling. Calling Gordon.

"Hey, I think this guy is a murderer."

"Lucie, it's fine."

"Really, there is no one here? And it is really creepy. And his office is in the *basement*."

"Lucie it is 7pm, of course it is empty. Just go. Keep your phone on and just call me if you get scared."

I proceed down the steps and at the bottom to the left there was a glass door. I can see a woman at a desk talking on the phone. The door was obviously soundproof. Even more freaky. I open the door and I am immediately taken back to 1972. No kidding. Everything was wood paneling. Even her phone looked outdated. I wasn't as scared now because she was here. I know there are three of us.

She gets up and brings me into a room that was possibly even older than the waiting room in its décor. The doctor walked in. He also was from 1972. Plaid pants, odd polyester shirt and a comb over. My body was screaming run, but I stayed.

Then nurse says, "Have a great night. See you tomorrow doctor."

Wait what? I pull out my phone. No service.

Panic attack.

He immediately asks me questions and I answer quickly. I want to get out of there and get my prescription for all the tests he does . . . but apparently this guy does the blood tests right in this office. WTF? Before I can even react, he was taking vials of blood from me. I swear he was licking his lips. When it was done, I could not excuse myself faster. He had to yell as I climbed up the stairs. He would call with the results.

I got home. And my brain started.

The doctor is a fraud.

What if the doctor is using my blood for something?

What if the doctor injected me with something?

^ That one stuck. (lol)

Panic attacks. It is 11PM by now. I wake my husband. I am freaking out.

"The guy injected me with something." I said it but did not believe it. Hard to explain.

"Lucie, he did not. You are okay. There is no way a doctor is going to do that."

"Sweetie, I know. Rationally I know. I honestly don't think that. But my thoughts are doing this weird thing and my brain keeps thinking it even though I know it's not true."

Gordon gets up and I hear the dial up of the computer being started.

He puts in the doctor's name and regurgitates all the info about him. He advertises he went to a top school, has been practicing for many years. No license issues. Nothing but great reviews.

"Thank you," I say relieved. I am okay.

The tests were normal. My thinking was not.

I didn't have a name for these thoughts. I really didn't have anything like this again for some time. I learn about these types of anxious thoughts later.

#whathappenedtomythinking?

25
My Comedy Act

"Laughing or Crying.
You still have to move through it.
I choose more laughter."

LONG STORY SHORT. MY JOB WAS NO MORE. I left one day because the panic was so bad and never went back. My body won. I went on short-term disability. Later on, I was denied long-term disability. Move on Lucie. I need to get better, not bitter.

One day I was lying in my bed crying. This was the norm back then, to be in bed, as I spent most of my waking hours there. I was feeling very sorry for myself at this moment and going into the "why me?" loop.

I was well aware that this is a victim mentality, I didn't do it often, but I was tired and worn down with malnutrition and anxiety. I was extremely underweight and eating limited food at this point. I was unable to go anywhere because I was literally allergic to the world. My room was the safest place I could be without reaction and it really sucked. My husband, Gordon, was by my side holding my hand. I could see the fear in his eyes, he clearly thought he was going to lose me. This made me cry even more and he asked:

"What honey, what is it?"

It was then I said through my sniffles, "I never had the chance to be a comedian!"

"You wanted to be a comedian?" he answered, with a half-smile on his face.

He then looked at me, as if to get permission to laugh. We both tore into a howling laughter. This seemed to heal the sobbing from just moments before and my sad tears turned to joy tears.

It was then I knew that humor would get me through all of it. I have no idea why I said that, not once did I ever think I wanted to be a comedian. I had worked in insurance for 16 years, the opposite of comedy. I can only imagine if those were my last words, how shocked everyone would have been. I mean I loved to laugh. Still do. But it was never a career choice. But now that I think about it, maybe it was. My job was to get well and to do it alongside of laughter. My audience was my family, friends and anyone I encountered. We all go through life's ups and downs; I chose to do it through the lens of laughter.

#laughtertherapy
#hilarioushealing

26
The Great Purge

"This is a small chapter.
To let you know how small my world had become."

EGGS. POTATOES. GOAT YOGURT. BOILED chicken. Olive Oil. Rice. = My food without reactions and what I ate every day. Only this.

Baking Soda = For my teeth and deodorant. A soap that doubled as shampoo = My hygiene products.

Stainless Steel cookware. No makeup. No smells in my house. Air purifiers. No vitamins. No medicine. Organic wood beds, mattresses and sheets. (This was tricky because it was before you could get organic everywhere.)

I went out only when I absolutely had to. Fake smiles to all.

Panic attacks and fear ruled my life.

Oh, and I was now a size small.

#iamdisappearing #theworldisclosingin
#tallgirl #smallsizenow

27
Energy is My New Buzzword

"Did you see the word buzzard there ^
Because I did.
I like to see things my way, no matter the reality."

I SAW A VIDEO ON THE INTERNET.

(By the way my computer smelled when I pulled up the internet. I could also smell the electricity from my computer. And the pesticides that were just put down on the house that was two over from me. All of this would make me shake and feel like I was going to pass out.)

They touched points on their body and went from sick to healthy.

Wait what?

These were peeps with anxiety and sensitivities. And they were getting well.

I wanted to get me some of that!

I could taste health. Or maybe chocolate. I wanted to taste chocolate.

I learned how to do it. I wasn't taking baby steps, but went in full throttle, tapping the shit out of everything. Me. My kids. My reluctant hubby. My dogs. Not kidding. We were all going on this crazy train. Yet, it did not feel so crazy. It felt right.

I started to spend money on coaches.

But there was always a reason I did not like each one.

That one was not smart.

That one didn't understand me.

That one was not certified.

Whatever they were selling I wasn't buying.

I was so cynical. My way. I know more than them.

Finally, I called the big man. No not God, that comes later (wait for it).

I called the guy that created the healing method. His phone number was on the website.

Why was his number there? Doesn't he know cray peeps like me will call him?

You would have thought I was calling Paul McCartney with how nervous I was.

But this guy was *my* hope. A healing rockstar. My hands were sweating, stuttering when I spoke:

"Um, yeah, um hello. This is Lucie. I love what you created. You are amazing . . ." and then a long stream of vomiting words that made no sense together.

"Thanks?! What can I do for you?" he said simultaneously sounding happy and confused.

"No one can help me. Why is it not working?"

"Work on why you think it's not working. And accept *everything*."

Hmmm . . . very Yoda.

I tried what he said. And it did work for a few things.

But not everything. I wanted to be done quick. Immediate.

I really thought it was going to be *the answer*.

I could get out of bed *a little now*.

I could take my kids to school *some days*.

But I was still having the panic attacks.

And still having the crazy issue with the smells.

And the silly problem that I was way underweight and not absorbing any nutrients.

#idontwanttodie

#makethesethingswork

#iwontgiveup

28
Shutting Shit Down

"Anxiety is like a puppy.
You can tell it to sit,
but it is going to jump on you
until you teach it to sit."

MY FAMILY AND I WERE ALL AT THE MALL. THIS was big news! I AM AT THE MALL!

Going out was a gamble, but after tapping every part of my body and even the car itself, I thought I was covered.

I was going to at least try. My husband unpacked the stroller and slid our youngest into the comfy ride. I held my older daughter's hand and she looked at me with a wide-eyed grin. She was so happy to see me out and about, you would think we were at Disney. My husband had my son hold onto the rail on the stroller and off we went. The five of us.

I am sure all looked normal to the outsider looking in. Young family going to the mall.

To anyone else, the mall is a place of shopping. To me, it was a place full of fear and obstacles that could result in me running to escape the invisible scents that caused havoc to my brain.

My husband watched as I confidently walked through the doors. Doors that I had not ventured through in some time.

Cue large department store.

I was walking around looking at the clothes and feeling pretty optimistic. I could smell everything and was a little dizzy, but nothing that would make me run. I needed new clothes because I had gone from a size 10 to a size 2 and my current wardrobe was being held up with elastics and ties.

My husband said my son needed to go to the bathroom. He grabbed his little hand and I watched them walk away. My girls continued to help me pick out clothes.

It was about 10 minutes later that I realized they had not come back from the bathroom.

My mind immediately went to danger. I raced to the checkout counter (my girls in tow) and asked, short-breathed and panic stricken:

"Where are the bathrooms??"

"The one's down here are not working today. You need to go to the second floor."

I clumsily raced up the escalator, stroller and all, trying to find the restroom. When I do, I have no hesitation to fling open the men's room door. I mean, it's okay when there is grave danger, right?

No one is in there.

I try to call him on my Blackberry. No answer.

Again. No answer.

Third time. No answer.

This is serious.

I casually (think yell like a lunatic) ask the man hanging clothes on racks if he saw my husband and son. He had not. This was not the answer I needed, so I continue describing them. Still nothing.

It was at this time that another employee came over and asked if he could help. I explained the horrific situation that was growing bigger and bigger in my mind by the second. I must have been terribly convincing, because now both of these men were joining in my fear party and calling for help.

I cannot remember exactly what I said to these men next, but something along the lines of,

"maybe they were abducted?" came out of my mouth for sure.

This sent the second man into a panic. One of my people I thought.

A manager came over and this is where things get fuzzy.

There were lots of questions such as:

- does your husband have any enemies?
- are you having marital problems?
- anything going on with your son we should know about?

This is getting big, even for an anxious person. But I thought they knew exactly what they were doing. I hear walkie-talkie type chatter. Police converge. Women begin surrounding me telling me all will be okay.

I am crying hysterically with complete strangers comforting me. The store is being sealed and locked down. I am being questioned by police while all my mind can think about is my poor husband and son that have been taken from me. Flashes of them in my mind show them on the floor of a storage closet tied up and struggling. Or maybe they were shot? Oh, please find them. This is terrible.

There are people stuck in the store. We are officially on lockdown.

No one can enter. No one can leave. I am on the second floor, by the escalators. Waiting. Crying. Imagining. It was the longest few minutes of my life.

I look up to see two figures, one tall, one tiny being escorted up the escalator by law enforcement.

The smirk on my husband's face as he was ascending towards me was priceless. It said everything all at once. There was annoyance, questioning, laughter, love and most of all understanding in his eyes.

I was greeted by the police with these words,

"Is this your husband and son?"

"Yes! Yes! Thank you! Thank you!"

And just like that it was over. I heard groans. Laughter. Cursing. Applause. Then, people going on with what they were doing before the abduction (that wasn't really an abduction).

Apparently, the bathroom upstairs wasn't working either, so they went into a store that allowed them to go there. My husband was rather shocked to be greeted upon his walking towards the store, seeing guns and an officer stating, "They fit the description."

He was shocked, my husband, but not surprised.

This is how bad the anxiety had gotten.

This is how my mind worked all the time.

I needed to find *the* answer to getting well.

#thisishowmybrainworked

#iwoulddoitagainbecauseiamscared

#actuallyididdoitagain

#shutdownawaterpark

#samestory

#differentbackdrop

#sameending

#helpme

29
Road Trip

"I was so skeptical.
But I thought I was dying.
Funny what dying will do to your skepticism."

ON THE INTERNET AGAIN. SEARCHING. LOOK-
ing. Researching. What was going to heal me?

Scroll—scroll—scroll . . .

Found it!

It was energetic imprinting on vials.

Somehow you hold the energy of the substance
that you are sensitive to and then in a few hours you
are no longer sensitive to it. This is a little to woo-woo
for me I thought . . . but then so was the dolphin healer.

Let me flashback to the dolphin healer. Just a week
earlier.

I think I paged her. She called me back while I was
picking up my kids from school.

I told her I would get back to her in a few minutes.

I heard the faint sound of ocean waves and squeaks before I hung up. This should have been my first (and last) clue this was not for me.

She actually magically called me back just as I was ready to call her. Huh.

She began talking to me about how to heal. She said you have to be happy for everything and everyone. Everything is love and that there is nothing else. All else is illusion. While I understood what she was saying, I could not understand how that was going to help me eat pasta.

She continued talking and really was filling me up with very positive thoughts and ideas. It was what happened next that threw me off guard, as she did not advertise herself as channeling dolphins anywhere in her bio. So, it was quite a surprise that she asked if it was okay if she went into dolphin mode. I felt compelled to say yes and for the next ten minutes I heard noises I had never heard a human make: loud, piercing clicking, whistling and squeaks that left me speechless. Although I am sure it was okay that I didn't say anything. I am certain it wasn't a conversation. I realized I had entered a world where few venture—going to all lengths and apparently all noises—to get well. After the healing, I had tinnitus for two weeks. I also began to eat mackerel and I am a much better swimmer than before (kidding). Just wasn't my cup of tea. I am sure it works for some. Enough said.

Now back to energetic vials.

This was like I said a little out of my wheelhouse. The only things I knew about energy healing were the few things I had done prior; the alternative doctor, the tapping and my porpoise friend. But the more I researched (anxiety gives you a love-hate relationship with researching. You want to know, but some of the stuff you find throws you into a tailspin of fear) the more I was open to try this.

Same pattern. I was like Goldilocks as I went to practitioners to help me.

This coach is too narrow-minded.

This coach is too pompous.

This coach is too *whatever*.

I finally found one that I deemed okay, but he was over a two hour drive each way.

Anything to heal. We made it a family affair. No joke. We would drive there. All got a treatment, sans Gordon. And then the circus began when we got home. My kids were game for this because they all had a few food sensitivities. Gordon was the guy who had to take care of us when we got home. Why? Because the rule was this: whatever you were treated with that day, you could not come in contact with or smell for at least 24 hours.

When we came in the house, we had to cover our nose and mouth with our shirts, running past the kitchen. You would have thought there was chemical warfare going on inside our abode and that it was life or death to sprint past the "bad guys" in my kitchen. We each swan dove into separate rooms because we could not come in contact with what the other was treated with.

Enter the plastic cooler.

We each had one.

Gordon would fill each cooler with the allowed food and/or hygiene items for each family member and he would hightail it from room to room making sure we were all set. For twenty-four hours, my husband took on the role of a nervous short-order cook, delivery man and energy blocker all at the same time. As crazy as it sounds, my kids got better. And I got a little better. I was making headway and I could feel it. A few foods back and I was able to handle a little bit more smells.

I wanted to know more. I needed answers.

I called the person that created this protocol and I flew out to meet her.

The plane ride out interesting. Think panic attack the entire flight.

But I was going to get well. I knew it.

She was amazing. She actually did a treatment on me there and I was able to eat a burger, fries and a soda that night. Well, she never told me I could have a soda, but I took the hit. WTF? This was heaven.

I was able to eat a burger after this—no bun, but I wasn't choosy. Burger was something new in my daily food intake.

#thankyou
#sograteful
#gettingthere
#stillnopasta

30
The Gas Guy

"Did you know your sense of smell
is heightened when you are stressed?
My brain actually rewired itself
for danger all the time now.
Even if there wasn't any danger. Or was there?"

I AM NOT SURE IF WE WERE FRIENDS OR ENE-
mies. Me and the gas guy. He certainly visited my
house enough times for me to think he must have at
least thought I was a nice woman.

Your sense of smell is extremely heightened if you
are dealing with multiple chemical sensitivity and extreme anxiety. My mom could no longer wear makeup
when she came over. Not kidding. And when my mother-in-law came over from Ireland for a visit, Gordon
explained she could not bring her beige foundation or
spray perfume. I loved both of these women and felt
so ridiculous putting restrictions on them, but if you
lived with me you would have understood. Gordon

understood. By the way both women tried, but I don't think really knew the extent of what was going on. Because yes, lavender is a scent and my mother-in-law spraying it to and fro around the guest bedroom does constitute a smelly substance. And Mom, you were not clever, I know you had all your makeup on.

It wasn't just makeup that was an issue, but I could smell heat and electricity. And I could especially smell gas. Natural gas that has no odor, yep, I smelled it. And when I did, alarms bells would go off inside my head. Think of the fire alarm that was triggered during a drill back in grade school, that exact ringing would begin as soon the odor reached my nose. The first time I panicked because I was certain we were all going down for the count. I called the gas company and they immediately sent over who I will call Gary (just because I love alliteration, I have no idea what his name was). Gary was well versed in all things gas and tried over and over to convince me I could not smell gas. Even on our first encounter, he was not buying what I was selling.

Gary: "Responding to a call of a possible gas leak."

Me: "Yes thank you, all I can smell is gas. It must be coming from the basement."

Gary: "You can't smell gas ma'am. If there was a leak you would smell the chemical that is in the product. Gas doesn't have a smell."

Me: "It kinda does."

Gary: "It would smell like rotten eggs. The chemical in the gas, if there was a leak"

Me: "This doesn't smell like eggs; it smells like gas."

Gary: "Impossible."

This little dialogue went on again and again every time Gary got a call to come to my home for a possible gas leak. This is why I think we must have been friends; it was always Gary. I mean what we the odds that it was the same guy every time? I think he was intrigued by me and somewhere inside himself he secretly thought: what if she is right?

It was on the fifth or sixth call I think I wore him down.

Because upon ringing my doorbell Gary said he smelled gas!

Hallelujah! He gets me.

I like Gary. But in all seriousness, Gary did smell something that day and was tinkering downstairs for at least 30 minutes. His gas meter thingy did not show anything in the house, but he thought maybe the rotting leaves behind our bushes in the front were creating some sort of gas smell and that we should clear it out.

After that Gary was not the responder to my house any longer, it was new guy. New guy was not as fun to deal with. I often wonder what happened to Gary. I think I may have changed his perspective a little to show there are no absolutes in life. And that sometimes you need to believe in the canaries.

#smellswereeverywhere
#panicandsmells
#smellsandpanic

31
What Is Safe?

"Grass is greener on the other side."

IT RAINED JUST BEFORE THE CONCERT. WE had lawn seats, so it was super muddy and impossible to sit down, so my hubby and I were just roaming around. I had been to many concerts throughout my years, but I was always the designated driver. Why? Because I had made myself a promise, after my sister's death, not to not do any drugs.

As an anxious person, this promise grew exponentially into a literal interpretation. Year after year more items fit into my "what is a drug?" definition. It began as just illegal drugs. Then certain prescription drugs. To all prescription drugs. To many herbs and even vitamins.

I think I may have been scared somehow that if I took a drug, I may die. My anxious thoughts consumed my brain with what could happen if I took a drug. So, even at times I would try a vitamin or an over the counter medicine, somehow my body created reactions to convince me that it was a bad choice and not to even attempt to try that again.

I would take a multi vitamin and literally you would have thought I took mushrooms.

No. Freaking. Kidding.

My daughter came home one day to ask what Tylenol was. I believe she was 14 at the time.

No. Freaking. Kidding.

There were zero medicines in our home. If someone had a headache or a stomach ache, the remedy was a glass of water and a hot water bottle.

So, at this concert and I am smiling in my tie dye shirt, jean shorts and flip-flops having an incredible time getting muddy and listening to music. But under the smile I was scanning. For trouble. For someone acting suspicious. For any sign of needing to run. Always on alert.

My feet started to feel funny from the mud and I noticed a rash forming rather quickly.

I yelled into Gordon's ear, hoping he could hear above the music "I have been poisoned!"

I convinced myself that it was the pesticide in the grass and it had invaded my body through my skin. Not only did I go to the emergency room that night, but for weeks following I researched everything about the dangers of pesticides. And know this: what you want to find on the internet will be there.

Pesticides is in my ever-growing list of drugs. It is banned. No one comes to "treat" our yard. We have neighbors with beautiful green weed-less yards. Sorry neighbors. Your yards really do look fab, but I like mine earthy-crunchy natural. Just the way God made it.

#sorryneighbors
#didyouknow
#dandelions
#cureshit
#andaregoodforyou
#trytea

32
Hot Mess

*"Over the mountain and through the woods has
such a different meaning to me now."*

WE LIKE DISNEY. MANY OF MY STORIES ARE
from Disney. Or from vacations. That is not because
we take so many vacations, but more so because it is
when you really can notice the symptoms up against
the "real world" and how anxiety not only has a hold
on you, but also the ones you love. It is also a great
reminder that many people are walking around looking okay, but in reality, they are a hot mess inside and
possibly barely hanging on.

It is so ironic that someone with debilitating anxiety, that can't even function, ends up year after year at
the happiest place on earth. But that was me. It was a
fence I straddled. On the one side was this completely
incapacitated fearful wreck of a person and the other
side was a fully present mom with Mickey ears on. I
often chose mom over all else; and that is why this
chick that could not even function, would get on a

plane to be with her family for vacation.

Don't get me wrong, it was a somewhat of a trag-ic-comedy act to do this.

I could not be near any scents or would freak. Cue perfume lady in plane seat in front of me. Or scented soaps and shampoos in the hotel room. I even side-eyed little kids at the pool that smelled like a box of dryer sheets, because I knew within mere minutes, I would be feeling panic. I learned very quickly to bring all my own shit and sit far back in the cheap seats when lounging at the pool. I also could only drink one type of bottled water and the park did not sell that kind, so I had lockers and frequent breaks at the hotel so I could get my drink on.

Anyway. They told me that it was just a tame roller coaster. Expedition Everest. I believed them.

I am certain they just wanted mom to have fun, but what went down on that ride, that day, is a piece of history in our house. The line was so long, but this is Disney. For some reason lines seem to work here, even long ones. I swear they must pump shit into the air to keep you calm because everyone is fucking grinning, even on two-hour long lines.

It was finally our turn. There are five of us. Always an odd man out. This time Gordon was in the car be-hind me with single-rider guy.

I shut my eyes the entire ride and blissed out into a meditation, trying so hard not to ruin this time with family. I take up so much time with the anxiety stuff, that when these moments do come, I work so hard to keep quiet. It was when the roller coaster stopped that I was a little perplexed.

I opened my eyes and we were stopped on the top of the "mountain". My kids had turned around from the car in front of me, looking at me and waiting. It was then I realized we were going to go backwards.

Let me stop here and explain my kids were young. I did not curse in front of them. They saw their mommy as a mommy that really was kind, gentle and sweet. But in the face of terror, I let fly:

"What the fuck is this!??? What the fuck is this?" Over and over again.

My kids roared with laughter as they watched me sink in my seat. Panic started and I wanted to unleash myself from my current location, but was stuck.

Cursing ensued.

Single-rider guy and my husband exchanged only two words and a chuckle:

"Wife?"

"Yep."

A chuckle.

As we spiraled backwards, I heard the sweet sounds of children gasping and laughing, alongside with my repetitive cursing and screams. I was sure I was going to die, but not from the ride.

It was the panic. Heart beating. Nausea. Visions of us all falling out and plummeting to our demise. And I swear I smelled a large waft of Axe aftershave during our descent, which made matters exponentially worse.

When we got off the ride, the kids were hysterical.

"Mom sorry!" Laughing.

"I never heard you say that." Laughing

"You okay hon?" Serious husband. He knew that this reaction could last for days.

We decided to take a little break to help my system calm down, so walking around the park to see the animals was a great choice. The five of us were excited to see the gorillas, so we stopped to take a look. We were lucky to get in front and right next to us was a tour group and their leader. The leader was speaking:

"This is a beautiful 450-pound silverback gorilla...." he began. We were all listening and very interested in what he had to say.

"... these Gorillas are very strong, almost six times the strength of a human ...."

I was so engrossed in what we were learning, that I realized I did not have my "mom radar alert scanner" going. I look around and didn't see my son. There are people everywhere crowding around this tour guide and I am frantically looking for my son. FOR MY SON. I check to the left of me, to the right; all within seconds. I have scoured the entire perimeter of the area and my kid is gone!

In those few seconds a movie played in my brain that resembled a horror flick. Kid gone. Person took him. Never to see him again. My body was trembling. My mind was whirling and I could not breathe.

The leader continued, "It is important we remain quiet. No loud noises, for we don't want to make the gorilla...."

The timing could not have been any more perfect if it was rehearsed. For out of my mouth at that exact second was a shrill, the likes that could shake a mountain.

"WHERE IS SEAN????" At the top of my lungs. I mean loud. Really loud.

People ducked. Gorilla looked up. I swear it made eye contact with me in a look that was like "are you stupid?" Gasps from the onlookers. Everyone frozen waiting for the next move. Apparently loud noises can make the gorilla upset and things could happen I guess if it was upset?

This all happened in seconds. My scream. Gorilla's glare. Frozen people. And getting a not-so-nice smirk from the tour leader that I deciphered as "great we are all going to be mauled because of you" stare. The panic within was out of control, but I also was quite aware what was happening outside of me. People were still crouched, as if being low down could shield them from the gorilla if it decided to somehow break loose from its habitat??

That is when my son came out from behind my husband's legs.

I ran and hugged him. People stood upright. Gorilla turned away. A couple weird looks. I don't care. My kid is back.

Sound familiar? A little like a story you have already read. Yeah, I know. All too familiar to me too. This was a big part of the anxiety, me thinking the people I love were going to somehow not be there. It sucked. It was all consuming. It took up space in my head and would not leave. And it played out so many times in real life. It was life draining. Anxiety blows.

LUCIE DICKENSON

#Peekaboo
#Iseeyou
#gorillasinthemist

33
Over The Bridge

"I may be sick. That doesn't mean I am stupid."

I DROVE TO ANOTHER STATE FOR A DOCTOR visit. A pretty benign statement.

However, it was quite an accomplishment for me. I didn't drive. I was terrified of driving on roads that I was not familiar with and I most certainly did not cross bridges. Bridges were non-negotiables.

Let me clarify, I drove my kids to school. To their playdates. To the grocery store.

(I tried not to go to the grocery store too much after seeing a woman on her own personal step ladder arranging the soup cans, with gloves on, so the labels were all uniform. It scared me.)

This doctor was a specialist that tooted his success with severe anxiety and chemical sensitivities on his website. I had to go. The sticky wicket was that Gordon could not miss work and this doctor was only open on weekdays. Gordon could not take another vacation day. There were so many times that man came home in the middle of his workday because of my emergency calls in panic. There were so many nights that he stayed up the entire night with me when I could not sleep. He had eaten up so many vacations days over the years. God, I despise anxiety.

Back and forth I grappled about this:

Driving four hours? Over a bridge and highways that I don't know?

Or staying stuck and possibly giving up an opportunity to get well?

To think about it was extremely overwhelming.

I got in my car. The panic already ramped up in my brain.

Pulling out of the driveway not so bad. Getting on the Turnpike, terrifying.

Hyperventilating. Heart palpations. Ridiculous thoughts and images.

I absolutely cannot stand trucks—tractor trailers driving next to me.

The steering wheel is wet from my hands and I am crying because I am certain one of the trucks is going to sideswipe me.

Many people pass me as I drive slowly in the center lane.

I won't go in the left lane—too close to the median.

I won't go in the right lane—too close to the edge.

Center lane. Slow and steady.

A guy passes me and gives me the finger.

Another one yells at me, "Get off the road!"

I am going 50mph. I am a hazard. It is the fastest I can go without completely losing it.

I get there.

I see myself in everyone sitting in the waiting room. We are all bones. Literally.

My turn. I walk in and he is smiling. Almost too much.

I don't like him. He was talking down to me. Said I needed to get it together and some other shit. Yeah, I know I need to get it together. Is that all you got? Because I can beat myself up for free. He knew I did not think he was all that. I could see it in his eyes. He was a manipulator.

An opportunist. On this journey I have met so many great helpers and I am so grateful. However, I have also met some not so nice people. The kind that take advantage of sick people. This was him.

He told me to put my pots and pans all outside in the sunlight for a full day and to only wear flowing cotton. I never said I had a problem with my pots and pans, but being anxious, I was thinking maybe I do? (Full disclosure, I only use stainless steel because I read something somewhere about birds dying from the fumes of some kinds of pans that were not stainless steel. We cleared out the cabinets and only stainless steel was allowed in our house, just in case. Fumes were a problem for me and I was a considered a canary, sooo . . .)

He told me some other stuff that had to do with ignoring the symptoms blah blah blah.

Yeah. I know. But what is the answer? There was

no answer. I wanted to be fixed. And there was not an easy answer.

I went home deflated. I almost didn't care about the ride home. I was even cooking back up the Turnpike at a swift 55mph. The bridge was a little problem, but I was so in my head it was nowhere near what it could have been. Isn't there anyone that can just give me the answer to make this go away?

#iwantanswers

#youcanthandlethetruth

#atleastnotyet

34
I Am a Super Hero

*"Oh, what a web we weave
when anxiety tries to deceive."*

I GOT BIT BY A SPIDER.

Not earth shattering.

And at first, I did not think twice about it.

The red bump on my arm growing.

Who else gets bit by spiders?

Surely everyone.

Spider-Man then popped into my mind.

He got bit by a spider. A radioactive spider

What if this spider had something in it?

I laughed for a second, then froze.

Wait didn't Spider-Man turn into a spider? Well not really. But kind of. Then the movie "The Fly" popped into my mind; and even though this was about a man genetically fused with a fly, the images from that movie of Jeff Goldblum slowly turning into a fly freaked me out.

Internet search: Many anxious people have irrational fears. Reading out loud:

"Oh, here is a man who heard the word werewolf and now is scared he is a werewolf." And

"Here is a woman who is scared of vegetables because she thinks she will be planted in the ground. Are you kidding?" These people are crazy, I think to myself (as I continue to fear my spider bite turning me into a superhero?? Lol)

Call to the counselor I was working with at this time:

"I was bit by a spider and now my thoughts freaked I may be a spider?? This is so stupid! But the thoughts keep turning up the heat. When I say to myself this is stupid, they just get worse."

Counselor:

"Yes."

Me:

"Dude. What is happening? I actually think I need to be locked up."

Counselor:

"Nope. You are fine. You are just extremely anxious. You need to give your brain the rest it needs. Lucie, here's an analogy. If you called me and told me you were scared your wallet was going to talk to you- that is probably anxiety. If you called and told me your wallet was talking to you and you were talking back to it, having a full-on conversation; then we would need to discuss things a little further about your next steps."

Me:

"Shit! I never thought about a wallet talking. What if I start thinking that? "

Counselor:

"What if Lucie, you are what if'ing...."

Me:

"I know. I know. This bite & Spiderman..." My counselor bursts out laughing. This makes me laugh. We chuckle for a bit and my thoughts calm a little.

Counselor:

"You are scared of anything hurting you or your family Lucie. It is understandable that you think anything that comes in contact with you is a threat. But it is not. Let's continue to work on what is underneath that. Deal with the pain, the grief, the anger, the forgiveness"

Me:

"Okay." Spiderman theme music playing in my head.

Gordon, being the most patient man in the world, listened night after night about how I thought maybe this bite was going to turn me into Spider-Man. He just hugged me. And held me. Until I stopped rambling and we would fall asleep.

Something people who don't have anxiety may not understand is this:

An obsessive thought can come into an anxious person's life and hang around for some time... but just like that it can go away.... mostly because something even more scary has taken its place... or because your mind releases it because it is no longer viewed as a threat... or because you used compulsions to quiet the obsession...

I did not want anxiety to be in control of the timing of when shit left. It was my time to not buy into these thoughts. I knew it would take practice and I knew that anxiety would try harder the more I ignored it, but I need to do this. I know it is bananas. These thoughts. But they are there no matter what I think. So, I am just going to let them be there... and do nothing about them. Not even fear them....

#spoiler

#notasuperhero

#but

#iam

#ananxiety

#slayer

35
Operation Stink Eye

"It is all perspective.
Did I spend too much and get us in financial distress
or did I spend just enough to keep me alive?
Or a little of both?"

WHILE I WAS ON SHORT-TERM DISABILITY, I was in a required class at the local community college. Getting to and from college was an event in and of itself. Most of my time was spent hiding in my bedroom but when I did emerge, I played the part of a healthy mom.

I would dress my withering body up and try to make myself look larger than I was. Baggy clothes and layers. Makeup was not a possibility because I was allergic to it all. Funnily, I had a complexion that seemed to get more and more glowing as these days of sickness rolled on. It was ironic. Here I was sicker than I could imagine, but my face and eyes looked ridiculously healthy. So, no makeup was an okay option with me considering the radiance of my face.

It was the inside that was calling for change.

I would race to the classroom so I could sit closest to the door, not because I wanted to escape but because of the amounts of time I has to excuse myself. This was due to the heavy perfume/cologne wearing individuals in the class. I would get migraines from the perfume and many times feel faint. The kids in my class (most were young kids) called me hippie mom. Not exactly what my intent in this life was to be known as, but it began to stick. I was that natural girl with no makeup that spoke up in class about toxins. We had to have a plan for a small business in this class and my plan was for a store that sold toxic free items and groceries. This may be the norm today, but I was pretty far out back then. I could not believe the person that I was becoming. I set out to set the world on fire. I was driven, was going to be CEO of a company one day. I had ambition and smarts . . . this thing that happened to me was morphing me into a person I could not recognize. Who was this person that now wore free flowing cotton (maybe I did listen to that doctor a little) and said no to food additives? Who suddenly was caring more about causes than being top dog? I wasn't sure. I wasn't even sure I wanted to get to know her. I was a stranger to myself.

It was towards the end of one class that I conjured up the nerve to call the people I had viewed in yet another video. A woman answered and gave me some information and the cost. Seemed a reasonable fee to heal at around seven dollars a minute.

I immediately knew after only a few seconds I was going to get well. I was on the phone with her for about 45 minutes. The fee was about $7/minute. Please do the math. I won't. I already lived through it once.

This began my phase of energy healing known as operation stink eye. I wanted to get well. I knew these people were going to be the catalyst for that wellness. But I also had the finance piece to consider. It was that piece that created the rift.

There is no way Gordon could have ever known the pain and the fear that I had inside. As much as I tried to convey my suffering, my tough resting bitch face self was never quite able to convey the level of pain I was in. I was born with this blessing (curse?) that I always looked strong and confident on the outside. No. Matter. What.

Someone in my family died? Look strong.

Family home gone? Look strong.

No money to go to college? Look strong.

I was the poster child for faking it on the outside until making it on the inside.

Except, it was no longer working. I'm not going to make it this time alone. I was out of chances and needed help big time. I would have done anything to get well. Hell, I did. I think I tried every imaginable healing tool known to man and porpoise, but I digress. I selfishly or selflessly, I am not sure which one to be honest, took the plunge and turned a blind eye to the financial part of this healing equation.

It was in those evening phone calls to the healer that I would sense his presence. He would begin by pacing back and forth outside the bedroom door. Gordon would never say anything and many times that is where it ended. Pacing.

He would hear my sobs into the phone and instinctively know I needed this more than we needed money.

But it was when he heard me laughing for minutes on end that I would get the stink eye. He could not fathom how or why I would be paying someone to get me to laugh. And even more so, in his brain, me laughing was parallel with me being okay, being well. He would get frustrated as the minutes ticked away and our bank account diminished. I called these healers for about one year, almost daily. Again, do the math.

I blissfully ignored it all. I knew I was dying. I knew I did not want to die. I needed this, whatever this was. I needed to live. I internalized and crawled within myself, blocking out the outside world. Self-preservation at its finest.

#myretirementaccounttookahit
#morethanahititwasgone
#icaneatfuckingpasta
#isntthatworthit?

36
It's Happening!

"Sometimes belief is learned in very odd ways."

I COULD SMELL THE VITAMINS, EVERY ONE OF them. It was an assault to my being. I would begin the panic upon entering the doorway and this would cause an alert in my head, but even more so, a heaviness in my heart. I did not run to escape though; I didn't have the energy for that.

I was slumped over while standing. My head held low. My emaciated frame dragged itself to the counter to get a green drink. I could smile and say, "please and thank you," but that was the extent of it. I could see people looking at me. That is okay. It was when someone said something that I would hang my head even lower:

"Are you okay?"

"Can I help you carry that?"

"Is there something I can do for you?"

I knew what I looked like. It wasn't a secret. The

exterior of Lucie was not a concern at this point. It was my internal world that needed some updating. For over a year I was a shell of myself slinking sadly into and out of this store. That is why my practitioner chose this as the first treatment. She said it would be easy proof that I could get better.

She told me after the treatment to go into the health store.

I was quietly excited.

There was a hesitation which was quickly replaced with hope.

I opened the door and there were no odors. There was no anxiety.

I straightened my back up to an erect position of pride, as I confidently walked down the aisle.

I inhaled deeply and was elated that this treatment worked. I didn't know how and I didn't care. I just wanted to bask in the light that there was a way out. That I was not stuck any longer.

Every day I would go back to this store. The first few times I was more than a little nervous that it was all a mistake and the symptoms would come back, but they did not.

Once one of the ladies at the check-out commented:

"Wow! You look amazing. I am curious, what did you do? You looked so sick and honestly, like you were not going to make it and now you look healthy!"

I was shocked she was so forward but I admired her for being so blunt. It was a reminder to me that I did not want to be in the position again. It wasn't about what I looked like, it was the energy I had been emitting.

One by one I tackled old beliefs and old outdated patterns of thinking. I brought out the grief and the anger that I was holding deep down and allowed the light to shine on it. It was a beautiful process. I began to believe.

I needed that foundation of hope. There were still smells that bothered me; actually, more than a few but I knew in time I would be able to overcome each one.

Each day I got a little better.

And then one day, I actually felt good. Normal. Not anxious. It continued for weeks.

#mommycangoout

#babysteps

#igotbetter

#yay

37
The Pirate's Life for Me

"Just when you think the storm has taken you down. You realize the storm was there to clear the way."

WE WERE HEADING OUT FOR A VACATION. A *family* vacation. The five of us. Six if you include the anxiety shit-ball. It came back with a vengeance. I thought it was gone. I believed it was gone. But its ugly presence haunted me with a cluster of new symptoms. Panic was now more a generalized, internal shaking every waking moment.

The smell issue was gone, which was miraculous, but a new sleep issue was beginning along with non-stop panic. My new normal had shifted a bit, but I was still full of fear and anxiety.

Gordon and I were not seeing eye to eye for the last few months.

We loved each other.

We just could not understand one another.

I had gone AWOL for a while and allowed anxiety to take my place as Lucie.

I made it my identity and my purpose became finding the answers to healing. I couldn't comprehend the fact that I had done so much to heal, spent so much money and I was back to square one. It deflated me. My faith was wavering big time. Why am I so weird? Like what is it about me that shit doesn't work the way it does for everyone else?

Gordon had also pulled a disappearing act because he could not understand the person I was becoming, so he just existed alongside of me. We both had changed. Or what he says now is that I changed. He was not there yet. He was not ready to make that jump with me.

Regardless, we both needed to learn about one another again.

Sickness. Disease. Mental Illness.

It changes you. Not necessarily for better or worse.

It is more of a gray area of not wanting to change, but forced to do so. And not at the same time. We were living side by side, but not together if that makes any sense.

It was this vacation that we were going to try.

We went to the Outer Banks. It was August and hot.

Three kids in the back. Hubby driving.

We got there and I could not even enjoy the hotel because my symptoms were so elevated.

Everyone went to the pool. I stayed in the hotel

room and curled up in the bed, lost in my obsessive thoughts.

Next stop was Ocracoke Island. You have to take a boat to get there.

You do not have to take a boat in a hurricane to get there, but hey this was me and my family.

We were the last ferry boat to go out that day.

We pulled our car off the boat and drove about half a mile before we came to a complete stop.

The hurricane had flooded the island. There was water coming up on both sides of our car. Not too high, but high enough. We sat for over two hours with no way to move, cars in front and behind us.

Gordon said he would be right back because the water was getting higher.

He disappeared behind the sandy hills toward the ocean.

Me. Waiting. 10 minutes. 15 minutes. 20 minutes.

Okay, he has drowned I thought.

The ocean has swept my husband away and I have nowhere to move and get my kids to safety.

(Did I mention I don't drive a car at this point because I am so anxious?)

I tell my kids to sit tight I am going to find their father.

My son is now in charge.

I run over the dune and down the beach. Waves are coming in high and strong. There is water everywhere and my shoes are sopping wet. I do not see my husband. I begin hyperventilating and panic consumes every part of my being. The feeling. The pain. I can't die. Lucie keep your shit together. You have three kids to go back to.

That is when I heard him. Not my husband, my son. I see a small figure running towards me.

"Get back in the car!" I scream to my son

"Is Dad okay??" he screams back.

This is when I see her. My daughter. Running out onto the beach.

The water is getting higher and I can't control this shit show.

And my husband has been sacrificed to the waves.

Wait? Who is with the little one? She is in the car alone right now.

I run to the two kids and into the car to find my littlest struggling to get out of her car seat.

I yell, "I told you to stay put!"

"Mom we just wanted to make sure you and Dad were okay," he says in such a sweet little voice.

Crap, don't want to create anxious kids. This needs to stop.

I need to find scuba gear and get my husband. I start crying. I love him. I can't lose him.

I look out at the ocean and see another faint figure. I run towards him. It is my husband.

"Where were you?????" I am so angry and anxious.

"I ran up the beach a few miles to see if there is a way out of here. It is one road in and out. There is nothing we can do. We need to wait it out."

Wow. That sounded familiar.

This was our turning point. Back to us.

I needed to accept the anxiety. All of it, so I could get back to our marriage.

He said he needed to accept that I changed, so he could get back to our marriage.

We looked at each other and knew,
just knew we were going to make it through this.
The storm.
Both of them.
#justminuteslaterweweremoving
#itwasagoodvacation
#anxietywasthere
#ididntcare

38
The Anxiety Trick

"Anxiety steals your peace.
You go from A to Z. There is no in-between."

"WAKE UP!"

"What? Are you okay?"

"Gunshots!"

Gordon went from sleepy to startled. "What??"

"Do you hear the gunshots?" I say quickly and louder

"Lucie, those are not gunshots."

"Really? Are you sure? Someone could be lurking around in our back-yard shooting things up. Are you certain?"

"Yes, Lucie. Go back to sleep."

What sleep I don't sleep.

And anyway, if I did, who could sleep with like five masked men in your back yard shooting up the house and getting ready to break in.

"Gordon! Do you hear those gunshots?" They were

getting closer. I didn't see anything out my window, but for all I know they could be army crawling right now. Getting ready to pounce on my family at any moment.

"Wait. I do hear something." I smirk at him. He looks a little concerned.

"Those aren't gunshots though. It doesn't sound like that." He gets up and looks out a few of the windows in various rooms. "Lucie it's all good, go back to bed."

My imagination is going wild right now. "Call 911."

"What? Why?" He is confused. I mean how could he be confused? I have already advised him of the gang of madmen outside our home, shooting for sport.

"Because we can be shot. Our kids are upstairs Gordon. Are you sure it's not gunshots?"

More than reluctantly my husband calls the police. He mentions noises outside the house.

I am screaming in the background, "Not noises! Gunshots! Please hurry!"

They converge. The police. Going in the back-yard stealth like. I am so happy they are here.

But they find nothing. No one. The noise stopped right when they arrived. Hmmmmm.

I am terrified. Make sure all windows are closed and locked. I know they found nothing, but I definitely heard *something*.

The next night I hear it again. The same sound.

I investigate because it is not dark yet.

This is when I see my neighbor hitting his golf

shoe against the deck to get all the debris off his cleat. *Thump. Thump. Thump.*

Mortified. But not really.

#anxietysucks

#worstcasescenerioalways

39
Bottoms Up

"Up your nose with a rubber hose . . .
or something like that."

LET ME START BY SAYING I TOOK MY HUSBAND along.

He also agreed to go through with this "procedure."

Not because he wanted to in any way, but because he really wished for me to be healthy again. We were now united. On the same page.

Gordon became my willing, but somber, sidekick in many of the crazy schemes and treatments along the way. He was the straight-man in this comical adventure of my healing journey. I secretly believe he loved being a part of this, as we really did make some incredible memories along the way, as odd as that might sound.

I had read on the internet (credible) that colon hydrotherapy would clean out my system and reset my digestive system. I knew way back then that there was a connection between my gut and disease, so I thought this may be a good idea. For those of you that have done this I am sure you are already laughing, because the experience in and of itself is beyond words.

Woman helping us: "You each have a separate room. Go in and get comfortable, take off your bottoms and sit in the hole in the middle of the room."

Glaring look from Gordon. I ignore and pretend not see him.

Woman helping us: "Unwrap the protective top right there and place it on the hose. Then gently move the hose into your body. If you need help just yell out, we are in the hall waiting."

Evil look from Gordon. I know I have to do something because he was a flight risk at this point.

I smile at him and shrug my shoulders. He knows this is code for we must go through with this, something has to help me get better. He smiles the smile that means I love you but also how did I get here? He retreats to his private room.

Entering the room, I am immediately confused. Before me is a hose and set up that resembles hole #5 at a miniature golf course. I proceed as instructed to the middle of the room and recalled in my mind her detailed directions on what to do. It was then that I looked before me and could not believe what I was seeing. It was a wall of glass front and center. Behind the glass was a quick moving current of water. My inquisitive thoughts were interrupted by the knock on the door.

"All good in there?"

My answer could have gone a million ways, but I was assuming she was asking specifically if I was ready for the hose to be unleashed.

"Yes," I answered, with gusto.

"Okay, I am coming in now." In she walked and thankfully there was a blanket that I was unaware of that she wrapped around me with care. She noticed me looking at what appeared to be an empty glass wall aquarium before me.

"Oh, so sorry, I forgot. Once you get started everything that comes out of you goes through there and you can see it flow by."

Wait. What? I began laughing to myself. Not because of what I was to see in a few minutes, but because I could only imagine what Gordon was thinking in his adjacent room. I was more than laughing, it was close to hysteria. The nice, helpful woman backed away slowly towards the door slowly watching my maniacal laughter ensue. Once she left, I turned on the power.

Interesting is an understatement. You have no idea what and how much is stored in your intestines. At first gross, but in time, I was actually cheering for what flashed from left to right across the glass. It took longer than expected, however I did not mind because I knew what was waiting for me outside. My husband.

We got in the car, without discussion.

I had the urge to belt out a catchy tune that popped in my brain about cleaning products, but I thought better of it. I watched him drive face forward expressionless.

I knew we would be howling about this one day, but today was not the day.

I bet tomorrow is. I actually feel lighter and better. This may work I thought.

I couldn't help myself I began humming six notes that brought us both to laughter.

#mrclean #mrclean

40
Tick-Tock

"Peels is Sleep backwards.
I figured that out while staring at the ceiling,
not sleeping."

"I AM HAVING A REALLY HARD TIME WITH sleeping."

"How hard?"

"I don't."

"You don't what?"

"Sleep."

She laughed. I wasn't kidding. There were nights I was up all night, and then again, the next night.

I thought it was a cruel joke that the universe was playing on me.

I conquered a few of the symptoms of anxiety and then did the deep work to release patterns and let go of chemical sensitivities . . .

And now this?

It made no sense. But to be honest, nothing made

sense because of the lack of sleep. I would go a couple nights and then pass out for maybe three hours, and then up again maybe a night, maybe two. No. Exaggeration. This went on and on for two months before I had to get help for my own sanity.

I found a sleep coach.

Had no idea these people even existed, especially back then. Coaching was not the explosive industry it is today and to have such a niche so long ago was surprising and gratifying.

Our conversation continued:

"Yeah, I understand. When I was having insomnia, I would get like 3 hours sleep a night."

She continued, "It was awful. I was told at a sleep study I was the worst case they ever witnessed," she said almost proudly? I didn't want to be in a competition with who has the worst sleep, that would be pointless and petty. But I win with zero.

"So, how can you help? I really would love to get some sleep," I asked.

When I said I would love to, I meant it. Not only was I speaking to this sleep coach, I worked on sleep hygiene (such a weird phrase for bedtime routine), caffeine intake, cell phone and computer lights, journaling, energy healing, and I hid the clock. I tried all the ways I could . . .

She responded, "Thank God for everything."

My new sleep coach went on to say when you thank God for no sleep, you are being thankful for everything in your life. This kinda-sorta made sense because it was similar to the anxiety symptom reduction plan—which was to accept everything.

So, while I was not sleeping in bed that evening, I raised my fist in the air (this dramatic pose was what my coach said she did and if it worked for her, good enough for me) and exclaimed loudly, "Thank you, God." I slept a few hours after that, but there was no real change in the long term. Another few months and the insomnia continued. I think God had another plan for me . . .

The plan was to friend God.

I really did not have a firm spiritual foundation as a child. The only thing I can remember from the few times I went to church was this: *Who is God? God is love.* If I was going to remember anything though, I think this was a good one to have stick in my mind. Because my sleep coach said I had to thank God, I felt I needed to get to know a little more about Him before I blanketly thanked Him.

To be honest, I was also a little scared of the whole religion thing. I saw a ridiculously scary movie when I was young. Like *ridiculously* scary. I guess my way to deal with those fears that hung around from what I saw in that movie was to ditch anything spiritual in my life. I wanted no part of it.

But it was time to release those beliefs from childhood and learn more.

I began to listen to Christian Rock and the Bible on CD. I got the Bible on CD as a free gift on my rounds for shopping a religion. Honestly. I literally had my hubby drive me and our three children around the county as we tested out several different places of prayer to see what resonated with us. I would listen to the CD as we were driving and half doze off on our journey of exploration. It soothed me.

The positive messages seemed to go beyond my conscious mind and sink into my subconscious. I felt like I was close to delirium from the lack of sleep, but would feel better when I closed my eyes and listened to the beautiful words and music. My soul not only loved the messages, it craved them. I had no energy to drive or clean the house. I did not cook meals. My husband picked up the slack for months. I was disgusted with my current state and my inability to do much more than exist, but it was these beautiful affirmations that kept me going.

I found a church where I felt I belonged. I got a sponsor and became a member. It was welcoming. The sense of community and the weekly services breathed a life force back into me that was lacking for some time. I became involved. I volunteered. I started to sleep.

What does this have to do with anxiety?

Everything. Because the insomnia was a symptom of the anxiety.

#mylifesong
#thisturnedsomucharound
#faith
#islept
#fyi
#istillhidetheclock

41
I Am Not Cooking

*"Everything you think of can be
turned around into fear.
I had to learn to turn fear around."*

IN THE KITCHEN, CHICKEN ON THE CUTTING
board.

Cutting a chicken for dinner.

CUTTING A CHICKEN FOR DINNER!!!

What is this barbaric ritual... cutting chicken?

My mind begins to race. Cutting. Chicken.

I look at the knife and suddenly it is no longer a
utensil, but a deadly object.

Mind whirls further.

Knifes are weapons.

I am holding a weapon.

WTF?

I am going to hurt someone.

I put the knife down and begin to cry.

Hearing my sobs, Gordon runs in.

"I am going to hurt someone!" I say though my sobs.

"What are you talking about Lucie?" He actually was a little stern with his response

"Look, I had a knife in my hand! What if I just start slashing everything, not just the chicken?"

"Sweetie, you wouldn't hurt a fly. Of course, you are not going to stab anyone."

"I might. Right? No one can be sure?'

I glare over at the knife on the cutting board and I feel fear rising up. My heart goes faster and I am dizzy. I try to look away, but I can't. My brain is hyper focused on the knife. I ask Gordon to please take it off the countertop and put it in the dishwasher.

I won't cut the chicken. I would not let Gordon cut the chicken.

The chicken is not cooked that evening.

The chicken is not cooked the next evening.

We throw out the chicken.

I am not sure if Gordon caught on, but I began making meals that did not require cutting.

I would be in the kitchen preparing dinner and the knives in the drawer would call to me. Not like I was hearing anything. More so like a knowing they were there, and that could mean danger. You know Edgar Allen Poe's the Tell-Tale Heart? How the guy freaked out after the murder and swore he could hear the heart beating in his floor boards? Well that was what the knives were doing to me- except I didn't commit any crime. The crime was anxiety. And I was an accessory to its warped lies.

Lucie, what if you lose your mind and start slashing everything?

Lucie, what if...

Lucie, what if...

I found stories on the internet about other people with OCD and anxiety that had this fear. Their therapy was to walk around with a knife in their hand. Exposure therapy. Fuck that. There is no way I am walking around my house with knives in my hand. So, I did what I thought was right. I threw out all knives.

That felt good.

But anxiety does not work that way.

You can't just throw out what you are scared of.

If someone said the word knife, I went into a fit of panic and I could hardly carry the conversation because crazy thoughts would bombard my brain. If I saw a knife on television, I would break out in a sweat convinced I was going to grab a knife and go on a rampage.

It took time for me to get it together on this one. Weeks. Possibly months.

I knew the more I entertained the thoughts the more my brain saw it as a danger. It was an easy statement, but so hard to practice. I went to Marshalls and got some new knives. I felt like a criminal buying them. I was sure that the cashier pushed a secret button under her register to alert the police Lucie was buying knives.

I brought them home and just looked at them. Creepy-scary freaking things.

I kept them in the package for a day.

Then they went in the drawer

Then I held one.

With every step my body wanted to run away screaming.

But I knew. I just knew that I needed to move forward and let my brain know there was not any danger.

It was amazing how I went from cutting a chicken to knives being a weapon in my thoughts so quickly. I knew if I was able to go from a normal task to crazy thoughts, I could go from crazy thoughts back to a normal task. It would just take some bravery and a whole lotta belief in myself.

Knives are no longer an issue.

But my brain was always on the lookout for the next perceived danger.

#chopped

#scaredthefuckoutofme

#buttheniovedtheshow

#itsallperspective

42
The Waxed Woman

"The ridiculous was normal.
Normal was out the window."

AS A WOMAN WHO COULD STILL NOT ENTER A salon or go to a gas station because of the fumes, I needed to get creative. Some things were easy at this point, like going to the grocery store. That I could do. But what about hair color or if I wanted manicures? Or even more importantly, waxing of my lip and chin. I once posted on Facebook these words:

> Dear Chin Hair,
> Cut the Shit.
> Lucie

Unfortunately, those unforgiving follicles of hair did not listen. When the sunlight hit me just right, I looked like a 17-year-old boy with the sprouting of a mustache and beard. I was sick, yes, but I certainly did not want to be found one day, in bed dead, with whiskers longer than my eyelashes. This girl had to find a way.

I had to use the closest thing to natural as possible, and even that in most cases would cause a reaction. There was a lot of do-it-yourself-attempts. There was this one time that I tried to do the waxing with a completely natural product. I had to microwave it and then use it immediately. This created quite a dilemma, because the freaking container that held the wax was literally on fire after heating it. Even with hot pads on, bringing this hot cauldron of molten liquid from the kitchen to the bathroom felt like my fingers would literally melt off my hands. Cursing loudly the entire awkward jog to my destination. This is where it got interesting. I would dip the organic wood spoon into the goop and the consistency would let me know if it was too hot or needed more heat. In between those two extremes was the small window of just right. It had to be done quick and skillfully. Both of which are not in my wheelhouse. I am not sure what happened this time, it is all a blur, so there is not an accurate play by play. What I can tell you is what I was wearing. I had on a sweater, and on top of that my husband's new North Face jacket. Because who doesn't do waxing in tundra clothing? In addition, I had on jeans and my new knee length black boots. What happens next is forgotten, as if I was really not a part of the incredible fight that happened between woman vs wax. What I can tell you is the scene my husband came home to after my teary emergency bat-phone call to him.

"I'm in here!!!" I hollered as I heard the front door open.

He entered and I could see in his eyes the "calmness in crisis" look I have become accustomed to. I watched him survey the damage as he leaned over and kissed me.

His new winter jacket was off of me and on the floor, looking more like origami than his North Face jacket. It was folded within itself, with multiple wax covered creases sealing it shut. My new boots had what appeared to be blonde stripes now. Obviously, again, the wax. There was wax stuck to the floor, which made walking a very tricky proposition. Standing still was key at this point. One boot survived on my foot, but the other was stuck to the murky substance about three feet from my body. The countertop was saturated with spilled wax which somehow made all ten fingers on my hands unusable. There was toilet paper strewn about, stuck to the counter and the floor. Think "ticker-tape parade after party" vibe.

The icing on the cake were my eyebrows. Or should I say eyebrow. I only had one now. It was while trying to contour these woolly mammoths that all of this went down. Again, it seems improbable, even impossible, but true. Simultaneously, as the wax spilled, I ripped off the dried wax on my brow and- abracadabra it was gone. Actually, it was mostly gone. There was a little nub that made it more insulting than not. I was a hot mess.

Gordon said nothing as he slowly took off my boot and led me out of the bathroom. He said I should rest as he methodically took out nail polish remover and began trying to right the wrong that just happened. I was so very thankful for his love and his help. I was also choking on the fumes from the nail polish remover, but I thought this was probably not the time to mention that...

#needtofigurethisout

#stuckathome

#literally

43
The School

"Fear or Love. What day is it today?"

I AM GRATEFUL FOR THE LITTLE TOWN I LIVED in. It is by the sea. There is such a wonderful vibe that pulses through the square mile of our close-knit community. Blessed beyond measure are thoughts that come to mind when I think of my town.

I never wanted anyone to know how anxious I was.

The school was the hub of everything. I loved that my children were part of the incredible experience that this amazing institution offered our family. On any given day these words could have either made me jump for joy or scare the shit out of me:

It's time for pick up.

When I felt good. Secure. Connected. Pick up was a wonderful time. I was getting better, so I had lots of good days now. I would park my car. I would get out of my car. I would socialize. I made sure to get there extra early to get a spot, to have time to talk with my friends and to make the kids playdate plans for the afternoon. It was a breeze. I loved these days. Our school was full of love and being part of the fabric of it all was therapeutic.

It was the anxiety days that creeped me the fuck out. It went something like this:

Get out of the bed I had been in all day. Put a hat on my head and sunglasses because I have not washed my hair, let alone my body. Park way far away from anyone. God forbid they see me like this. But there was always that one person that found me.

"Lucie, Lucie . . . is that you?"

Me reluctantly lowering passenger side window.

"Yeah, hi . . . hello? How are you?"

Person who never talks to me except when I am like this:

"Are you going to the meeting tonight?"

Shit. Forgot there was a meeting. Mental note: shower necessary.

"Yeah, see you there." Begin raising window. Panic is ensuing. Heart pounding. Weird thoughts. Dizzy. Even a simple interaction could throw me into an attack.

Apparently, my anxiety is like a dog whistle because everyone seems to now be crowding around my car. The car I parked way far away from others today is now the center of the social scene. Great. Acting as normal as possible. Do they know I am having a panic attack right now in front of them while I am pretending to take a phone call? I always try the phone call scheme hoping that they all wander to the next car in line and let me have my moment.

One friend would jump in the front passenger seat. Another in the back. All talking and laughing. I join in, but my laughter is at the irony of the situation. I pray my laughing will create an invisible force field around me that encloses the stench of not showering. I tell them I am busy today which is a really not a lie—I am busy wrestling with this beast called anxiety. They all file out of my car and I watch as they go into another.

I cry. Just a little.

For the person I wish I was.

For the things I cannot do that they can.

For the fight I am in and can't get out of.

For being a little jealous of them.

I want it so bad I can taste it. Freedom.

#hellokidshowwasyourday

#mommyisjustgoinghometorest

44
Stop the World,
I Want to Get Off

"Anxious Peeps Take Words Literally.
Even if those words are on a recording. On a ride."

CURLED UP ON THE THEME ROOM BED, AWAKE. Full of racing thoughts and visions of dying. This was another Disney experience. As morning light came, my bleary-eyed self, shifted from tired crazed lady, to sneaker-wearing ready for action mom. Because what else could I do? I happily mustered the strength to put on a smile and ventured out to the parks with my hubby and three excited children.

Somehow the kids convinced me and my husband to go on a ride called Mission Space. I do love me some rides, but anxiety had held me down and would not allow me to enjoy the park as a participant too often. Anxiety reminded me there was danger in the rides. Especially after the roller coaster incident from a few years before. For much of this trip, I sat outside the exit area, waiting for my family to emerge with grins and stories of their fantastic experience inside.

So, yeah, I approached Mission Space with the trepidation expected when approaching something like- I don't know... clowns emerging from the forest??? My heartbeat was already elevated as we followed people in a long zig-zag line. I rehearsed excuses in my head for why I must leave this line and not ride this scary contraption. The thoughts would come in and tell me to run, but I stood up to my fear this time and said to myself:

"I will never get this day back with my kids... it's time to level up Lucie."

I had been tracking Brian. He was one of the kids that worked on this ride. I know his name was Brian because his name tag told me so. He was also from South Carolina, also on his name tag.

I made a mental note of it all- just in case.

We were ushered into a room where we got directions about our mission. I was shitting bricks.

There were lots of words that were freaking me out, but one word stood out like wildfire.

Hyper-sleep.

WTF?

Heart pounding. Dizzy.

Before I could object, we were then shuffled into our spaceships and I was now in full panic.

As we sat down, I noticed the front panel dashboard of our spaceship. I immediately imagined smoke coming out from the vents, filling our vestibule with sleep inducing drugs. Hyper-sleep was necessary for the many year journey needed for us to get to complete our mission. At least that is what we had been briefed to believe.

"BRIAN!" I scream.

My kids laughing.

"BRIAN!" I yell even louder. I am half crying. Half laughing. But fully in panic.

"Brian, please come. I need to get off this ride. I don't want to go into hyper-sleep.

"Please Brian hurry. I am losing ground. I am going to pass out."

A little commotion. I see my husband in the spaceship next to me. He is with my daughter and I know he sees me being ushered out of the ride, leaving behind my two other children. He looks a little confused, as his door gets sealed shut. But, come on. He could not have been that confused. He knew what was happening. This was not our first rodeo.

As I stood there in the room that was filled with just employees and me, I felt so alone. I was escorted by Brain and another fabulous fella to an exit door. An exit door that did not seem to be there before. I am certain I would have noticed an exit door while planning the possibility of an escape. I would not put it past the mouse to have had this built in mere seconds just to happily get me off the ride smiling. The mouse is extremely smart.

Of course, I didn't really believe Disney was putting us in hyper-sleep. It is the overwhelming barrage of anxious thoughts that tell me to run... just in case. It sounds so silly and so believable all at once.

As I sat at the exit once again, waiting for my family, I knew I needed to get this shit under control. This time though, instead of beating myself up, I realized I took baby steps and I was almost on the ride. Next time. There will be a next time. And that will be the time I make it all the way through.

Brian is now my family's code word for when mom needs to escape. We all giggle just a little when it is said.

#Brian
#Thankyou
#Nexttime

45
The Hospital Loop

"The better I got, the harder I fell."

EVEN THOUGH I WAS SEEING PROGRESS, ANXIety has this habit of barging into your life just when you think it has left. So emergency room visits were a thing.

Like I should have had a frequent visitor card and get points or something.

There were a handful of times I thought I was having a heart attack. There was the time I was carried out of work. There was the time my husband and I were suspected to have been roofied (you will read that one soon!). There were a few other times with odd symptoms and stomach issues.

And there was one time at band camp. Kidding. There was one time even on vacation.

I would sneak out mid treatment.

Hide the nitroglycerin pill in my pocket.

Throw the medicine in the garbage when they were not looking.

Didn't they know I couldn't handle medicine?

I learned not to say that. The first time I spoke up and said I couldn't take medicine,

I was asked, "Then why are you here?"

I *didn't want* to be there. I *didn't want* medicine.

I just *didn't want* to die.

Here is an example of a flashback emergency room night:

"I feel like I am going to die!!!!"

"You doooo?" The last word was drawn out with the beginning of concern.

"Yes, I am sweating and it won't stop. I am drenched. Soaking. Please help me." Not sure if I was really talking to him or anyone or anything that could hear me.

"You really feel that bad?"

"So bad. Please what should I do? I am shaking and my heart is going too fast. It won't stop. I think I am going down. I am going to die." The last part probably inaudible because of my tears.

"Go to the hospital. Get off the phone and go. Just go, now! Call 911."

I called the ambulance. I was on a medication for an infection—a UTI. The first medication I had attempted to take in years, but I was told I had to, my third day in and this is what happened. A reaction.

^ This poor guy I was on the phone with was an energy healer that specialized in trauma, anxiety and probably after me, hysteria. His coworker called me the next day and told me they were not going to charge me for the session. That he was shaken by me. Heck, I was shaken by me. I was not faking. The things that were happening were real. There was just no evidence of it in any of my tests. It was invisible.

Wish I could take that power, that strength that I invested in my fears that scare not only myself, but others and turn them into faith. Faith that there is a greater calling for me. That I am not someone that is supposed freak myself and others out. To harness that energy and transmute it into something more. I decided to have a conversation:

"Hello God. Are you there? It's me, Lucie." (Who else prays like this after reading that book??)

If I got an answer I was going to vomit, so I continued before I could hear a reply. "I know there is more for me. I just know it. Help me see it. And when I do, I will help others see it."

#faith
#faith
#faith
#luciehavefaith

46
Lollipop Guild

"Trusting life was so hard.""

I BELIEVE PHONE TRACKING WAS A GIFT FROM God directly to me. This may sound overly egotistical but hear me out. I think God was throwing me a giant bone to help me get better.

"Mom I am so excited. Thank you for letting me ride my bike to school."

"Have fun kids. Make sure to look both ways when you cross the streets."

They got on their helmets and looked more excited than I was when I saw Duran Duran for the first time. I watched as they literally leaped onto their bikes and began to pedal down the driveway. I yelled "have a great day" and then I sprang into action.

Starting the engine of my car was not the plan, but there is never really a plan with anxiety.

It is spontaneous and cray-cray. I drove down parallel streets. I timed it perfectly so when they came to a cross street, I was also just approaching that same cross street and could peek out to see them.

To make sure that they were both together. Following the rules.

Who am I kidding? I was making sure a guy in a white van had not pulled over, luring my kids with lollipops into his lair of creepiness. Think the Child Catcher in Chitty Chitty Bang Bang.

Sweat pouring out of me. Fears they would not be there when I approached the intersection. Quickly it would all flash in front of me. The images were horrible and tough to watch, but I was forced to look, because I could not escape my own brain.

But as I looked over, full of panic, instead of a white van I saw kids smiling as the wind met their faces. They were happy. Free. Loving it all. They were perfect. It was me that was a little nutty, day after day, waiting at cross streets to make sure they were good.

I knew it was wrong. I knew that I needed to trust. Trust life. Trust the universe. I just did not know how. I questioned everything and saw the worst outcome in my head. It was on about their tenth ride, that my kids told me they knew I was following them. They saw me lurking through neighborhoods and although they did not tell me to stop this ridiculous behavior, I just had to. Because I wanted them to know I trusted them; it was the rest of the world I was fighting against.

This is when they got cell phones.

Another tough one for me. Because cell phones were going to scramble my kids' brains like eggs from the radiation. Right? A quick internet search led me to these little buttons I could stick onto phones that protected their fragile eggshell minds (thank you Mr. Mojo Risin).

Not only did I stick these suckers to their phones, I had them on our computers and our televisions. I also began to sell them because I thought; how the fuck could you have any electronic device and NOT use these??? This was about twelve years go. It was a little out there. But I was pleasantly surprised peeps were buying them from me. It was my side hustle. My true job was getting myself straight and to stop the anxiety somehow.

I told them to call me when they got to school. Those ten minutes were the longest ever. My imagination would play the greatest tricks on me and sometimes (most times) I would give in and still case my own children. It was ridiculous. I needed something to wean me off being a complete psycho. Because it was pretty evident, I was looking like the Child Catcher; driving slowly down neighborhood streets. Honestly, surprised no one called the cops on me.

But then God gave me a gift. A phone tracking app. I could find my kids

WTF? This is amazing!

The peace of mind was exhilarating.

What was even better? It helped me take small steps in the right direction.

I would only turn it on to make sure they got there.

And then, with more time I learned to ask them to call when they got to school, without the app even on. I would only look at it if they forgot to call.

And then finally, I stopped using it to track them riding to school. I needed something to help me trust and this literally fell out of the sky.

#smallsteps
#biggains

47
Another Dimension

"It pains me that some people believe OCD is just
about putting things in order.
That is perfectionism people, not OCD.
And I was dealing with both.
And it should be CDO, just saying."

EVEN THOUGH I WENT THROUGH A PERIOD
where the anxiety seemed to simmer down, I learned
it can wax and wane, especially when you are experiencing high stress. I guess I was now in high stress?

At this point, anything I thought of went into a
filter of lies that churned out warped thoughts in my
head. I remember someone mentioning something
about a guy on drugs who thought he was in another dimension. They were laughing. I was not. I went
home and obsessed.

My frigging brain latched onto this:

- What if there is another dimension?
- What if I get caught in another dimension?

- What if I stay scared forever about another dimension?
- What if one of my kids goes into another dimension and I never see them?
- What if someone secretly gives me drugs and I go into another dimension?
- What if the people on drugs are right and there is most definitely another dimension to get lost in?

It sounds ridiculous but to me, in that moment, I was dead serious. Of course, I KNEW I wasn't going to go into another dimension. However, it was the fear and the what if thinking that plagued my mind. It was on an endless loop that would not stop.

I approached Gordon cautiously with this one.

Casually, I asked him, "So, what do you think about other dimensions?"

I actually thought I was smooth with this approach. That he would not see through my words as being elevated anxiety. I thought I was in the vein of "So, what do you think about the color of my sweater?" talk, but he saw right through me. He knew at this point how crazy this had all gotten.

As I asked him, my mind was racing and I was sick to my stomach. I could not bear the thought of being in another dimension, away from the people I loved. I was having extreme muscle spasms and shaking in my body. There were tears in my eyes because my brain would not stop churning and churning the thoughts of going into another dimension. It seemed so plausible and ridiculous at the same time. While I knew sanely this was anxiety, it overruled my sensibilities.

The only thing that would help me get through this was an answer. I was in obsession/compulsion mode. The obsession was the fear of being in another dimension, the compulsion was to find an answer that satisfied the obsession and would quiet it down.

So, I did what any anxious person would. I Googled. Shit, it says there are people who actually have been to other dimensions. Anxiety is now even worse, but I know the drill. If I can find just one article or comment where someone can convince my anxious brain there is no other dimension this will stop. I keep reading. Crap, did you know that aliens are thought to be from other dimensions? What if I am an alien trying to get back to the correct dimension?

Lucie, get off the internet.

Gordon tried to help. Whenever I mentioned going into another dimension, he would break out into his best robot dance, moving his hands in rigid back and forth motions. He would then sing in a monotone voice "another dimension." This would make me laugh for a moment. He would then hug me and many times I would feel better. Sometimes though, I thought what if I am in another dimension right now and so is he . . .

Finally, after a few weeks of this I found an answer that quieted my mind. (For the moment.) It was some silly comment that mentioned rather officially that we are all in the dimension we belong and there is no crossover. For whatever reason, this one worked. And the obsession stopped.

This was not just a one-time occurrence or subject matter. This was a daily occurrence of anything I saw or heard that my brain could scare me with. I rationally knew that the anxiety was trying to protect me. What I could not understand was if it was protecting me, why was it trying to scare the shit out of me to the point of driving me to feel like I was going over the edge or needed a drink? Yeah, yeah, yeah, I know flight or fight . . . the anxiety is trying to get me to make a move to keep me safe from danger. I am starting to call bull on this.

Maybe there is something more to this?

Is all of this anxiety?

Or is this anxiety plus? It is such a blanket word—anxiety.

When the symptoms are not understood and they resemble a cluster of symptoms that point towards anxiety, you get labeled anxiety. But I have been through anxiety a couple times and this is much different. I am lost because the way out the last two times is not the way out this time. Anxiety is a slippery little sucker. It morphs. Like a shape-shifter. Or bacteria. Or Jell-O.

#ocdstinks

#pureo

#sometimescompulsions

#losingweightagain

#thisiswhathappenedatthevampiredoctor

48
Drink Up

"First it was the solution.
Then it became the problem."

I LIKED TO HAVE A COUPLE DRINKS SOCIALLY.

However, it was when I figured out the anxiety stopped when I had a drink was when wine became a game changer.

I didn't need the wine. I didn't crave it or have it every day.

But when I was shaking, or in obsessive mode I could have one or two glasses and I felt relaxed. The symptoms just stopped.

This was very convenient because it was around this time my kids were in school and I began meeting parents. We all began hanging out. They knew very little of my struggle with anxiety and I only shared bits and pieces, mostly through poking fun at it and keeping it in the past tense. I learned if I had a couple glasses while with them, I seemed to fit in. I was able to laugh and engage in the conversation instead of worrying about the obsessive thoughts that were barraging my brain.

There were many times I would decline the invite and stay at home or retreat for weeks because I was trying to get rid of the OCD that was now the norm. But if I chose to go out, I made sure to have wine so that I could level the playing field and enjoy.

But . . . In time, it no longer worked. After a few months of this I had the exact opposite happen. After a glass of wine, I would wake in the middle of the night with anxiety with my heart racing and I would be up for hours. After going through the insomnia fiasco, I knew how important sleep was, so I ditched using alcohol as an equalizer.

#alcohol
#isnot
#ananswer

49
Intruder Alert

*"'What if' are the two scariest words
to an anxious person."*

I WAS IN THE THICK OF IT. I HAD BEEN LIVING alongside this anxiety monster on and off for years.

I felt like a failure because I had already been through the energy healing a few years ago and now here I was lost, again. Why did this come back?

At this point my lifeline was my counselor.

He was prolific. We had many phone calls. This is a made-up call that summarizes many things I learned from him. This is how I remember it if I were to smush a bunch of the calls together and really get you to the meat of what I learned.

"Hello, hi I have so much to talk about today."

"Okay."

"What the heck is this crap that is happening in my mind."

An understanding giggle from him. The reason I

chose him to help me is because he had ridiculous anxiety at one point in his life. He got it.

"I am having thoughts that take over my regular thoughts. Like invading my mind."

"Intrusive thoughts. Yeah those are scary."

"Like all of a sudden a thought pops in: *What if I go crazy?? What if I just lose control and start running around doing weird things?*"

"Yep."

"And then the thought gets legs and it turns into more like *I am going to lose my mind.* But the weird part is there is another part of my brain that is rational and knows this is not what I am going to do. That it is not what I want."

"Yes, it's the anxiety. It is telling those lies again."

"Well that little fucker is getting louder and louder. I try to remove the thoughts but they keep coming harder. I don't want them. It is driving me to think I am actually going to flip out."

"You actually are not. In fact, you are more in touch with reality than most."

My turn to giggle. If this is reality, I want to go back to a fantasy world.

"You see you are so entrenched in the now you get lost in it instead of merely accepting the present moment and the thoughts that came with it."

"I know I know. The less I entertain the thoughts, the less power they have . . ."

I begin to cry. Really hard and then begin talking. An inaudible cry-talk.

He waits.

". . . it's just, just, I don't want to go crazy why the hell would I ever have *that* thought in my mind?"

It was then he said the most beautiful thing I had heard in years, "You know why you have these particular thoughts?"

"Because I am nuts?"

"Because it is what you love the most."

"Wait. What?"

"Anxiety has this vicious talent to take the things you most care about and creates something awful from it. For example, a parent who absolutely loves their children could have anxious thoughts about hurting their own child! These thoughts are repulsive to them and they freak out and try to rid themselves of the thought. Which only makes them grow. But when they understand it is anxiety doing this and not their desire, they know to ignore it and the thought dies."

"So, you are saying I love life so much? I value my life? That is why I am having *what if* thoughts about losing it?"

"Yes. Anxiety takes what you most love and is doing all it can to get a reaction from you. The reaction is needed, anxiety believes, so that you can be ready for all perceived danger. It thinks there is danger and it will do whatever it can to get you to be alert. The very fact that you are freaking out and don't want the thoughts is the very proof that this is not your intent."

"That kinda makes sense. Warped, but I can work with that." Immediately I felt my shoulders relax. And the noise running around in my head slowed for a moment, as if to pause and take note. But then the anxiety ramped up again. Why?

Thoughts started going through my brain:

- Okay, I know now my sanity is just what I love.
- Are you sure?
- Maybe he just said that.
- Maybe anxiety is now going to make a move to show me that he was wrong.
- Of course, you are going to end up strapped in a straitjacket in solitary confinement.
- No. These freaking thoughts. STOP

This was a typical scenario. My mind would focus on the outlandish and absurd.

But, with time and a little faith what he told me worked.

These thoughts stopped by me just letting them be.

I had these thoughts so many times, like with the 1972 doctor and the "another dimension" thinking. It was great to have an answer. I love answers.

#gettingstronger

#whatifsucks

50
That's Amore

*"It wasn't giving up or giving in.
It was simply giving.
To myself. Health."*

I WAS REALLY EXCITED TO GET PIZZA BACK. And pasta. While I was on a healing protocol, I was taken off all gluten and dairy.

"Can I eat a slice of pizza yet??"

"Let me check."

Let me check meant a mysterious process of checking to see if my body would accept pizza.

It was yet another form of energy healing that I tried.

"Yes. You can have one slice. And do not have any more."

I chose to hear *I could eat a whole pizza.*

"Round up the family! We are going out for pizza!!!!!"

Cheers from the kids as they jumped up and down

for their mommy. And to be honest, I am sure they were more so jumping up and down for them. Our house was strictly organic and mostly gluten free. Back then you could not go to the store and get gluten free organic anything. And what you got at the health store was a far cry from tasty. Now a different story. Then crap.

I ate. Have you ever watched *The Meaning of Life*? When the guy explodes eating? That was me. Could have been a whole pie. Could have been two. Not sure. I was doing my happy dance.

That night though.

Anxiety attacks.

Panic.

Weird crazy thoughts in my head.

Racing thoughts that would not stop.

Going and going.

Nah that wasn't the pizza.

Try again a week later. This time only one slice.

Same shit.

Try pasta. I love pasta.

You're kidding me.

When I hear people talk about their gluten sensitivity, they talk about digestive issues.

The way gluten issues manifested for me was in my brain.

And the more I ate it, the worse it got.

I would get a rash first, followed by anxiety for days.

I had to give it up.

It was like a death. I am not even kidding you.

Food was so engrained in me (silly pun) that I actually mourned it.

I learned that I had leaky gut.

I did the protocol to heal my gut.

Over and over.

Gluten just wasn't in the cards, even with my gut doing better.

I have dreams about pizza.

About Vic's baked penne.

But feeling good was more important so I chose my brain. My mental health.

The day gluten left the picture was when the intrusive thoughts vanished.

Another piece of the healing puzzle.

^ I wish that said another piece of pizza.

I learned when you take something away, it is smart to fill that space with something loving, so you do not feel deprived. I was obviously getting the message that nutrition was a large part of healing. What did I want to add in? Green drinks. I would get them every day. And with each day I got better. Stronger. Faster. I was like Steve Austin.

There is something to this nutrition thing.

#feelingbetter

#alittlepissed

#itsokay

#nutritionispartofthesolution

51
Seeing the Light

"Making it happen feels amazing."

LOOKING BACK ON ALL THE HELP I GOT, I BE-
gan to see a familiar pattern.

Just like in childhood.

I thought I was broken and needed fixing.

Even one of the well-meaning energy healers said
to me early on in my healing quest:

"Yeah, you are just too sensitive for this world. You
are like a canary in the coal mine."

I felt small when she said that. What I heard was:

- You are too sensitive.
- You exaggerate.
- You are an overreactor.
- You should disappear.

I was always looking for someone else to do the fixing. I took what everyone said and internalized it and

made it my world, my reality. It was them that had to fix me and it was me that would react to their findings.

It was now time for me to take responsibility for it all.

I felt a little like Glinda. You know:

"You've always had the power my dear. You just had to learn it for yourself."

So, I took that shitty perspective and I turned it around.

Heck yeah, I *am* a canary in the coal mine.

So what? I am sensitive. It is because I am able to see the imbalances in this world.

So what? I react to food and chemicals. It is because I am one of the people that can help warn others of the additives in our food and the toxic environment.

So what? I have *what if* thoughts. It is because I am so very empathic, grounded and connected.

Thank you, lady energy healer, for calling me a canary in the coal mine.

It is a gift, a gift bestowed among the helpers and the healers of the world.

Taking ownership meant looking within to see what needed to be adjusted for health, but also accepting what was as my gift from God.

Moving forward I was going to see this all as a gift.

- I began writing a blog.
- I began a business to help others.
- I began getting certifications.
- I created an anxiety protocol.
- I began getting better.
- I began exercising.

- I began eating healthy for me.
- I began meditating.
- I began practicing gratitude
- I began connecting.
- I began believing and having faith.
- I began daily prayer.

The love I found for myself was the catalyst for healing. I was creating an environment my soul loved.

#yougogirl

#thebiggestthingidid

#wastolovemyself

#nomatterwhat

52
Dreaming Awake

"What does this mean? Is the new question.
No longer is it: What is wrong with me?"

I WENT A YEAR WITHOUT ANY SYMPTOMS OR issues.

My mind was clear.

I was able to eat most every food I wanted. No problems.

I had no fears about my family disappearing any longer.

The scary thoughts during the day stopped. Well, aside from the normal *I am a mom and my kids are growing up and how do I do this parenting thing?* . . .

The OCD was gone. No more panic attacks. No feeling scared and jittery.

No more scanning for emergencies and the feeling of doom.

It was replaced with joy.

But then it happened.

Maybe it was just a fluke, I thought, but it continued night after night.

I would climb into bed and when I shut my eyes, pictures would begin flashing in my mind. Not just any pictures, horrific pictures and they were going in a really odd sort of avant-garde film sort of way. Clips of pictures hopping from one subject to another quickly.

I learned these were nighttime racing thoughts. Mine had a twist of something called hypnagogic hallucinations along with the racing thoughts.

It went like this:

- I would nod off to sleep.
- Thinking about whatever.
- Then suddenly somehow a video begins playing (or CD, MP3 depending on your age) in your head.
- You have no control and you are forced to sit and watch.

It literally felt like torture. The subject would be scary images and acts that made me want to vomit. It would happen right before I drifted off to sleep. Sometimes I would have the added bonus of intrusive thoughts on top of this.

"No!" I would scream. Startling my husband to jump from his sleep.

Opening my eyes, scared to shut them again.

But I am tired.

Eyes shut.

And it begins again.

A woman in a beautiful dress being shot.

Cut to a man in a grave, walking bloody and moaning.

Cut to a child scared and lonely.

All images and people I don't know.

As all these images were fluttering back and forth, a loud thought (not a voice) interrupts the mind movie, and it would go something like this:

YOU NEED TO GO IN THE ATTIC AND CLEAN OUT THE VEGGIES!

Would flash in my brain. What? It was non-sensical banter that would go between images and loud thoughts all night until I fell asleep. It was jarring to say the least. Especially after years of no issues. This would go on, night after night, for weeks.

Thankfully I had the power of belief in myself at this point. I knew from my training in nutrition and energy healing, this was a symptom, not an issue in and of itself.

I went over what I was eating.

I wasn't eating sugar. Or gluten.

I didn't eat either of these because through trial and error I found that sugar was a contributor to my panic and gluten was pretty much the reason for my OCD.

Although I loved my pasta, I loved my health even more.

But I did still have a daily cup of coffee and loved my dairy.

It was like a switch. The day I gave up coffee was the day that these horrific images stopped.

When I told my counselor (he was on speed-dial

from our sessions the year before, and I called him about this) he chuckled. And I immediately knew why. I was not supposed to be drinking any caffeine. It was part of our initial agreement when we began. But I thought I knew better. That caffeine was not a part of the problem. I did not have to follow his rules and he would never know it. It was the "aha" moment for me that the rules were not about him being right and me being wrong. The rules were not a power play. The rules were for my own benefit, for me and my health.

I miss that delectable cup of hot happiness. It was my morning affair. I loved her. She apparently did not love me.

Sometimes what looks like anxiety can be a sensitivity.

Or sometimes what looks like a sensitivity can be anxiety.

That is why overreacting has many meanings and anxiety is an umbrella word:

- Sometimes overreacting is your body talking to you and letting you know what it does not want.
- Other times overreacting is just that, an overreaction.
- And still there are times that it is truly anxiety and the adrenaline is an overreaction to perceived danger.

Understanding the differences was my lesson. #overreacting

#notabadword
#somuchbetter
#learningmore

53
A Quick Jaunt

"Listen to yourself. You are smarter than you think."

MY HUSBAND IS FROM IRELAND AND HAD NOT seen his family in years, so we booked a trip. The kids were so excited to see their Granny! While there, we had the idea to go to Paris. To get on a plane from Dublin to Paris was *very* cost effective, almost scarily so. I think we got round-trip tickets, for the five of us, for well under $200 total. This was one of those no-brainer decisions.

We were only in Paris for 24 hours, on Valentine's Day and I had our family packed with sights, activities, and French cuisine. Oddly, although only one day, it did not feel rushed at all.

We started at the Louvre and worked our way through the streets of the First Arrondissement, to the Eiffel Tower, pastries on the street and bought locks for the bridge after a cruise down the Seine. Perfect right?

Time for supper at a beautiful restaurant.

"I will have the duck . . ." (OMG on my first attempt on typing this line I had the letter *i* where the *u* is supposed to be. I could not stop laughing for five minutes. Juvenile, I know.)

I added, ". . . medium well please."

In an almost undecipherable accent our waiter shot back, "Don't you dare! Order it rare!"

I curled my face up with an unapproving look. He took that as a cue to keep up his attempts to convince me.

"The best dish in our restaurant is the duck. And if you want to experience the best French cuisine, rare is the way to have it. There is no other way."

Against my intuition, I ordered the duck, rare. I ate the duck, rare. (I hope they were using stainless steel). The duck that was almost too tough to cut through and honestly, I was worried the poor thing could possibly still fly off my plate. He kept coming by saying it is superb and their best dish, so I followed his lead by consuming the entire plate.

The next day we were in the airport and I suddenly felt a pang in my stomach, that quickly turned to sharp pains, so bad I could not walk. I was so nauseous and had to find the nearest garbage can to emit what was ailing me.

I was pacing back and forth, dizzy and sweating, running to the bathroom at Charles de Gaulle airport. I thought I was doing to die in the stall.

It was certainly the rare duck. (By the way the letter swap thing happened again, and just as funny this time.)

My daughter came in to check on me at one point and I hollered to her.

"Fly home without me. I am good. I will catch a flight later." I meant it. I was not going anywhere; I was that sick.

I listened to what this waiter wanted instead of what I wanted. This guy doesn't know what I want. I know what I want and need.

I had time to think about all of this while sick in the Paris potty. So many experts through the years told me I had to do something one way or could never do something another. I learned when someone uses the words always and never these were my clues that it was probably bad advice, because there are no absolutes that accommodate everyone.

And not only was I told I needed to do these things, I was told how much, where and how. Yes, some of those recommendations were my ticket to get on the path of healing, but there were many suggestions that were worst things for me. Such is life; trial and error, it is how we learn. But I have a built-in guidance system, my intuition, that I needed to trust. It was time to trust.

Anxiety helped me see that. Hmmmmm.

#listeningtome

#oui

54
Two for the Price of One

"A little insight into the anxious mind from another point of view."

A LITTLE WINE. A LITTLE CHEESE AND CHOCO-late. A beautiful night with my husband and friends at an outdoor comedy show. We get home. Hug the kids. Say goodnight. Off to bed. Nothing out of the norm. I was so much better at this point.

That is why waking up suddenly at 3am was not expected. The room is spinning. I have never had vertigo like this before. This was literally the craziest feeling ever. I was covered in sweat and I was complete-ly disoriented. Danger alarms that had been silenced for some time, were chirping and happy to ring in my head again. I wake Gordon and say I need to go to the hospital.

I went to the bathroom and felt completely sick.

Gordon goes into the bathroom to get himself ready to take me.

This is where it all takes a turn. Actually, not a turn. A nosedive.

I run out to the car and jump in the passenger seat. Sick as a dog.

Gordon comes out, but looks weird.

He falls to the ground right between the front step and the walkway.

"Gordon!!!!!" I scream

He is showing signs of not breathing too well. His hands are clutched to his chest and I am not sure what the heck is happening.

He puts up his finger, as if to say "One minute. Let me catch my breath."

But he is not catching his breath. He keeps holding up his finger and gasping.

I normally am a whiz kid in these scenarios. Because anxiety has helped me be a freaking rockstar during emergencies. Emergencies are my jam. But here- in this situation- something was off. I picked up my phone to dial 9-1-1 but my brain did not seem to be working. I could not comprehend how to take my finger and place it on the number 9. It wouldn't work. It was surreal. I knew I had to call but my brain and body were not functioning as one and I just could not dial the number.

I begin crying and yelling "I am sorry" to Gordon. I don't know what is happening.

He begins to crawl slowly towards me and is gasping for air.

It looked like a scene from The Walking Dead.

No this is not a dream. This shit Is real.

I keep trying to connect my hand to the correct numbers and somehow, finally I get through.

Boy would I love to hear the recording of what I said to that dispatcher. I know I said something along the lines of I think we were drugged and my husband is dying please come quick.

Within seconds there were two ambulances and police in front of our house.

The police mention possible carbon monoxide. Super mom appears. I get my shit together very quickly and run into the house to wake up my kids. They come out groggy and confused.

I am then escorted into an ambulance.

Gordon in the other. The kids are with my husband. He is immediately put on oxygen.

I am freaking because my family is in the other ambulance and I am not sure if Gordon is okay.

Wheeled immediately into a room, Gordon in one adjacent to me.

He is given a drip and still on oxygen.

But I am just really worried about him.

Lots of blood tests.

Lots of questions.

They checked for drugs and everything came back negative.

Doctor said it could have been a drug that they did not test for?

Or that was already out of our system?

We were interviewed and asked where we had been.

And if we left our wine glasses at any point?

They were perplexed. The doctors.

Not us. We were not perplexed. This seemed like a Tuesday from back in the days with anxiety.

If you can't imagine what anxiety is like; have you ever been drugged and your mind is hijacked? Well, there you have it then...a small glimpse inside an anxious mind.

I would like to say this was one of the oddest things that happened to us, but that would be untrue.

#hijackedminds

55
Role Reversal

"Very clever, God.
You had me see both sides of it.
Thank you."

THE SEATS COULD NOT HAVE BEEN CLOSER ON this plane.

When I say tight, think sardines. We were traveling to Iceland on a budget airline.

I was on the aisle seat and Gordon was packed in the middle next to someone who seemed to be wearing his entire wardrobe on his person. We suspect he was trying to get around the one bag rule. Body heat in our row was an understatement.

It was a big anniversary trip and one of the few vacations I had taken without our kids. We were pumped to have this time together without our third passenger: anxiety. It had been years since I had dealt with anxiety, aside from the occasional adrenaline rush when I allowed my stress to get too high. It felt great to have let that go.

Settling into the flight I thumbed through a few magazines I had bought in the airport and eventually relaxed enough for a nap. It would be about four in the morning when we landed, so I wanted to get a little sleep before we hit the ground running in Iceland.

About halfway through the flight, Gordon nudged me awake.

"Hey, I have to go to the bathroom. I feel so sick."

"Okay," I say as I begin the impossible task of moving in my seat. I had to unfold my legs, arms and torso in a contortionist fashion to allow my husband to get into the aisle. I noticed he looked a little sweaty but I thought it was spillover from garment-man. It was dark, so I switched on the overhead light so I could kill time reading until my husband's return.

That is when I heard a thump.

A couple running flight attendants flew by me and gasps.

I peer over my seat and see them all huddled over something in the front of the plane.

WAIT. My husband is in the bathroom at the front of the plane.

No worries. Nothing happens to my husband. He doesn't faint. That's me. Or at least that was me. You know the overreactor.

But when I look again, I see the bathroom light is vacant and no sight of Gordon. I should have known something was up because my hubby is not a public restroom guy, like ever.

Crap. I make my way to the front of the plane and sure enough it is my husband passed out on the floor, right between the drink cart and the garbage. There is white residue all around his mouth and I am like what the heck happened in three minutes?

"This is my husband," I say quite officially to everyone and no one, all at the same time.

"Okay, we just put this sugar packet in his mouth with a straw." One of the attendants says.

"Okay." Why did I say okay? What does sugar have to do with my hubby on the floor. I guess she saw my face because she continued.

". . . in case he had an attack and was going into a coma?"

I am even more confused now but they obviously did what they had to do.

He begins to come to and my first words were not the best choice but I said them anyway . . .

"You better not die on me mister. We have a vacation to go on and a life to live. No dying allowed."

He forced a small smile. I felt completely helpless. I couldn't do anything to make it better. While I was having this Kodak moment with my hubby, one of the attendants got on the phone and *the* announcement was made.

"If there is a medical doctor or nurse on board, please make your way to the front of the plane." It was right out of a movie. Two women came forward, one a doctor, the other a nurse. They briefly checked him out and thought he may need some food. One of them had two granola bars in her hand that she seemed a little hesitant to hand over. Like I said, this was a budget airline so the food you had was your meal for the duration. They talked with him for a few minutes and told him to stay put for a bit on the floor.

I then had my turn with him. He looked awful. Pale. Sweaty. Wearing white crystals on his face that would make you think he just did a plethora of drugs. I wanted to make it all okay, but kept my concern to myself because I did not want to upset him.

"Hey honey, you okay?" I said chomping on the newly acquired granola bar the medic finally handed over. "Want some?"

"No. And yes I am okay." He answered with a small giggle. We talked a bit more, he seemed good.

"Want me to stay and hover over you?" I asked while being lightly pressured by the flight attendants to get back to my seat. It felt weird to leave my sprawled-out hubby on the floor at 35,000 feet in the air, but I was not allowed to be blocking the aisle. I am assuming at this point Gordon is not considered a block, but more a temporary fixture of the plane's floor. People will need to step over him to go to the restroom. Such is our life! Life? Life.

"No, I am good, go sit down."

I shot him a look of love and assurance. The same look he has given me many times through the anxiety years. It was interesting being on this side of the events for a change.

I went back to my seat and felt concern and love.

What I did not feel was anxiety. Interesting.

After about forty-five minutes he was escorted back

to the seat. Gordon was now in the aisle seat and I was next to Mr. Snuffleupagus in all his glorious clothing. Boy was I hot. Gordon looked better and we now were getting the rock star treatment. We told them it was our anniversary so I guess that, coupled with passing out, entitled us to an entire bag of marketing yummi-ness: champagne, chocolate, socks of which I wanted no part of (clothing was taboo at this point), coupons, a stuffed animal, and a few other odds and ends.

We left that plane without ever having to say we now know what each other felt like in our roles over the last 15 years. It was a blessing and a turn of events which gave each of us more empathy for the other.

#twosidestoeverycoin

#wowwhataflight

#sothankfulallwasokay

56
Wheels Up

"What is the first thing that came to your mind when you thought you might die?
It certainly wasn't your child's grades, your dirty house or what's for dinner."

BLESSED FOR ANOTHER ADVENTURE. GORDON and I got to go to Sedona for a quick vacation. It was on the way home from this fabulous experience that things went a little south. Before it even happened, I knew. I have that talent. Except for the lottery, not sure why my sense of knowing doesn't work for picking numbers. Whatever.

The plane descended towards the airport and the hair on my arms stood at attention, as did my internal radar. At this point in my life anxiety is pretty much like a distant relative that I only see on major holidays, and even then, it's a crap shoot. But on this plane, during this landing, I knew there was a problem.

I didn't hear the wheels come down. You know

how you hear that? Well, I didn't. And that further freaked me the f out. I was in the middle of three seats across. Gordon had the window and to the right of me was a young man, around college age, with earbuds in. I looked at Gordon, who looked calm as a cucumber, and I said calmly:

"The wheels didn't come down." I was keeping the anxiety at bay. For the moment.

"What? They did."

"Nope," I said. It was here, the pivotal moment . . . when I could either doubt myself as I always had or believe what my gut was telling me. I chose guts.

Then I heard the familiar noises that sounded as if wheels were being let out of their compartment. Then I heard them again. And again. Three times I heard the noise, but each time there was a piece of the recognizable noise pattern that seemed to be missing.

The rest happened rather quickly. We were mere feet from the landing strip and suddenly the plane's nose shot back up in the air. Silence is an understatement. I felt the familiar pangs of anxiety. Sweating. Fast heartbeat. Thoughts racing through my mind so quickly I could not identify all of them.

"What's happening?" I ask quietly to my self-proclaimed aviation expert husband.

"I don't know." It was not his response, but the concerned look on his face that scared, no, terrified me.

"Walk me through this Gordon," I said with tears in my eyes.

The pilot interrupted our cheerful conversation with this:

"Sorry folks. There is debris on the landing strip so we have to reroute and get permission to land again. Thank you." Anxiety has taken over. I panic.

"Gordon, the wheels didn't come down, did they? Debris on the runway? Is that real or is it the wheels?" He says nothing. I can tell he is thinking, deeply.

I continue, "Gordon. What happens if the wheels don't come down? Can we land? What happens? Sweetie, I want the wheels to come down." I am getting a little louder at this point and my neighbor to my right has taken off his earbuds and looking my way.

My thoughts have become my words. "Shit Gordon, can we land?" My neighbor is now rubbing his hands furiously back and forth and turning red. I scan the entire plane. There are other people looking nervous, but there are also those who are calmly reading, talking and laughing. WHO ARE THESE PEOPLE??? I mean the wheels didn't come down on the PLANE YOU ARE ON . . . and you are calmly going about your business? Don't they care? Didn't they listen for the wheels or do they just trust the pilot's "sorry folks . . ." statement. To me the pilot's statement seemed very John Candy-esqe in a "Sorry folks, park's closed" nonchalant kind of way.

We are back up in the air at this point. Gordon goes into technical mode.

"If the wheels don't come down, we can still land. We may go over water to dump any excess gas first and then try to land."

WTF? Neighbor appears to be crying. Slow tears begin dripping down my face too. I look around and there are now a good number of passengers freaking out.

"I want to call the kids. It is not letting me call the kids. I can't call the kids." I am furiously playing with my phone trying to connect the call.

"It's okay." Quietly. Reaching for my hand and grasping it tightly. Looking into my eyes with such love.

"No, it is not. I want to call the kids. I need to tell them I love them."

"They know," he says touching my face.

It was like a bolt of light came down and hit me just then. My whole demeanor suddenly changed. In the past I would have continued to freak out, but I surprised even myself with what I did next.

I put down the phone.

I snuggled into my husband and told him how much I loved him.

And I thought. I thought about my kids. I thought about my life. I thought about God. I thought about how blessed and grateful I am. I was calm. I was happy. I was okay.

I had zero control over this situation and I was good with it. I settled in for the next ten minutes and just loved—me. my husband. my kids. my family. my life. —it was such an amazing feeling.

Then I heard the most beautiful sound ever. The wheels came down and within minutes we landed. Cheering, happy passengers. To this day I don't know

what really happened. Even my hubby, who rarely in-
dulges in my incredible imagination, agrees with my
version—that the wheels did not come down on the
first pass.

I was changed forever.
I was okay with no control.
I was okay with acceptance.
I was okay—no matter what.
#changedwoman
#wheelsonthebusgoroundandround
#wheelsontheplaneshouldgoupanddown

57
A New Perspective

"There is that moment in time
when it all comes together.
And you can connect the dots."

MY KIDS ARE GROWN NOW.

When I look back at videos and pictures sometimes it amazes me that I was able to do what I did. Through all of the anxiety I was able to be a fully present mom to my three children. I volunteered. I was a room mom. A scout leader. I was there for all their sporting events and academic programs. I studied with them. I cuddled them. We went on vacations, and I dropped them at friend's homes. I may have done this with extreme panic pulsing through my veins, but I did it. I love my family.

I also was very open with them. I communicated, probably sometimes ad nauseum. I told them what was happening every step of the way, obviously without trying to scare them, but I am sure I did. I wanted to stop the cycle of not talking. I needed them to know no matter what, I was okay. It was okay to have a mental illness. It was okay to not feel good. And it was okay to try so many different ways to get better. I also wanted them to understand that I was doing my best. My best vacillated from one day to the next and that was okay too.

I taught them about belief, about inner strength, about love.

I told them failure was temporary and one of our greatest lessons.

There are so many lessons we taught one another and we grew to understand the importance of those lessons.

I can remember calling home the first time I was able to eat a burger without any anxiety attached to it. My oldest daughter answered the phone.

"Guess what? Mommy just ate a hamburger!"

"Yeah Mommy!!!! You are so strong, Mommy."

"Thank you, Kitty."

"I love you Mommy."

I made a promise to myself, years ago, when I saw my kids standing at the emergency room entrance. I saw their frightened faces watching me, their mommy, being wheeled out of the ambulance and into the hospital. I vowed right then and there to not let anxiety stand in the way of my family and that I was going to be the best parent I could. I did both. At least I think so?? They may write a book one day that spills the tea on how they really felt in our toxic-free, fully organic, positive space, only non-violent video game house.

So now they are grown. My children.

This past year we went on a vacation, all five of us.

We had the opportunity between points and good fortune to stay at the Ritz Carlton. My kids had their own room and they were psyched to have the opportunity to come and go as they pleased to the theme parks, while my husband and I enjoyed relaxing by the pool.

The first day Gordon and I lapped up the sun, the drinks and the service.

I don't mean to make this a commercial for the hotel, but hell yeah! It was amazing.

We spent the next day on rides, watching shows, meeting up with the kids and finally ending with a great meal. We got back to the hotel and within minutes there was a knock at the door. We were handed wrapped gifts, compliments of the hotel. WTF? I was really enjoying the luxury of this hotel. I had been so used to financial problems from childhood and because of the cost of treatments to get better, we had always been somewhat frugal with our planning. Not saying we didn't travel, we did. But we worked hard to get it all into a budget that worked for us.

Anyway, enjoying the hotel

. . . and I need to go to the emergency room.

Did I mention I had a UTI on this vacation? It was only the second UTI I had ever had in my life.

But sometimes it takes two to make a thing go right. It takes two to make it outta sight. (A little Rob Base rocking the microphone? lol)

I knew I was hot. I didn't think I was that hot. I could tell by their faces something was wrong.

"Get her in a room now please."

I heard things like:

Extreme elevated heart rate.

103.5 temperature

and code sepsis.

I looked around trying to find the unfortunate soul that matched those symptoms, but I was the only one in this part of the building. They took me immediately to a room. Fucking great. It's me. I am spending every point we have earned on a luxury vacation and I am in an emergency room.

In came my nurse. He was a rough around the edge's kind of fella. Straight talking and no bull.

"So how you feeling Lucie?"

In walks a woman while he is speaking with me.

"A little hot. But okay." I am smiling and laughing. The woman shoots me a strange look.

"You must have some ridiculous tolerance for pain," she says, almost looking to see if I am real. "Because you are on sepsis alert right now and obviously have a raging infection."

"Yeah, pain doesn't really bug me. So, what is going on with me?" I say looking back and forth between them both. My nurse begins an exam to see the level of pain in my kidneys. I tell him it hurts a little when he gives me the soft karate chop to my back.

"I have only had a few sepsis patients. They all died."

Gordon shot him a look of disbelief. Obviously, this guy did not understand social cues because he spoke up again.

"Most don't come back from it."

I wasn't going to listen to this guy. I think he had an odd sense of humor and was actually trying make me laugh. I just ignored him and listened only to my results, which came back positive for a kidney infection and swelling. I needed to be admitted.

I was telling jokes as the EMT's rolled me out of the satellite emergency room.

"Can you guys stop for a few seconds?"

"Why? Are you okay ma'am?"

"Yes, I just want to feel the sun on my face before I get into the ambulance. This is my vacation and I was looking forward to getting some sun and relaxing." They laughed. I was freaking serious. I wanted to hang at the Ritz. And play golf. And go out on the lake.

The ride to the hospital was surreal. I had been in this situation more times than I want to admit, but this was different. I was calm. I got into my new vacation room/hospital bed. It was nothing like the Ritz, but it would have to do. I was given intravenous medication for the infection and told to rest. I am not sure what else you can do in a hospital, but I shook my head in agreement regardless.

The kids went to Epcot and bought me something from each country and brought it to me at the hospital later that evening. They thought it would make me feel like I was part of the vacation just a little. I loved that they were sharing with me this way. And that they were making the best of the situation.

The next day I thought I would be released. No such luck.

Another round of antibiotics.

I was in good spirits and so grateful for the hospital. The doctors. The medicine.

All the things that were helping me get better.

That night, all alone staring at the hospital room ceiling, I began to see the irony of it all.

I let out a chuckle.

This was bigger than an infection.

This was my second chance. My second go around, full circle.

Here. Here in this hospital I saw it so clearly.

I remembered trying to convince that healer, way back when I had my first UTI, that I was dying and I ended up in the hospital scared and anxious.

But this time was different. Yes, I was in a hospital. Yes, I had a UTI, but I am not scared one bit. I don't think I am dying. I know I am going to get well. There is not one ounce of anxiety. I even have a nurse that is trying to tell me I might die, but I don't take his bait.

Huh.

I began connecting the dots.

The irony of peeing on someone and now having a UTI. Hmmmm . . .

I peed on someone. I was showing the world I thought life was just a big piss party.

But now, I have a UTI infection. Interesting.

Life is not a piss party, that was infected thinking. And that thinking is coming out.

Or the fact that I used my entire life savings (and then some) on healing. I wasn't sure if we would ever recover, but here we were in the Ritz Carlton, in two rooms. Well maybe not me, because I am staring at the ceiling in the hospital room, but my name was certainly on the registry. We recovered financially. And I got well. It did not need to be one or the other. I could have both.

How about the fact I was given crazy high doses of medicine in this hospital? I never thought I would be able to handle any medicine, let alone being mainlined with a syringe full of the stuff, but here I was getting better because of it. Sometimes medicine saves your life, but many times it was the worst thing for me and my body let me know. I now know the difference. The belief "things work differently for me" was bullshit. I just needed to understand not everything is an absolute, even medication.

Or that I spoke up and advised that I wanted to discuss my options for not staying a third night. I felt powerful, not powerless any longer. There was no anxiety. No fear about the choice. Just facts and discussion that led to my eventual release that afternoon.

I thought I was broken for many reasons. But I was never broken. It may have felt that way, but it was just the process of becoming who I was supposed to be. Yes painful. Yes scary. Just like a caterpillar who thought life was over, I rose from inside the darkness and emerged with wings to carry me through the wind. Wherever the wind may take me.

This was all too amazing and coincidental. The more I thought about it, the more parallels kept coming forward to show me how far I have come and how I had overcome.

Especially overreacting.
I had overcome that.
I was now over reacting.
#mystory
#ablessing
#thankyouanxiety
#miraclesareeverywhere

Part 3

The Lessons

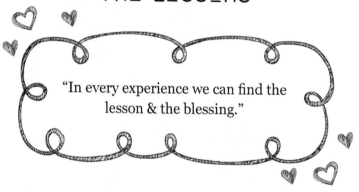

"In every experience we can find the lesson & the blessing."

I was once asked by someone
Dealing with extreme anxiety
How do you help yourself stay clear
of anxious suffering?
I paused and simply said.
"The lessons & love."
Nothing more needed to be spoken.

58
I know. I know.
Not Self-Help.

*"Sometimes the exact thing
you think is not your calling
is the very thing you need to do."*

IT IS MY BELIEF THAT THE FINAL STAGE OF healing is using what happened and what I learned to help others. My intention was not to make this a self-help book, but a memoir. However, while writing the first two parts, I realized the book would not be complete without the lessons I learned.

So like Obi-Wan Kenobi, I wave my hand in front of you and say:

This is not the book you thought you had.

Maybe you were looking for a flashy ending, but if you remember I told you in the introduction—this is not that book. I do not have all the healing complete and tied together with a big red bow. (I actually do not know anyone that has all their healing complete and if someone tells you they are done with their life's work; they must be dead because we are all works in progress.) There are layers in healing and in growth. I think I have peeled back many of the bigger pieces, but I am certain there are still more layers to uncover. Today I am a much healthier, happier lady who is just as much of a hot mess as anyone else.

What I do have is a bountiful toolbox overflowing with coping skills and lessons.

In this next section you may notice a repeat of the same message. Great. That is intentional. I cannot tell you how many times I needed the same lesson to be repeated to me over and over again. I was surprised by myself because I would not learn in one go. (Perfectionism sneaking in . . .) I would be hit by a 2x4 again and again and still not get it, but eventually I did. Mostly. To be honest, I still have days and nights that I forget what I have learned and I get stuck. But today, I get out of the hole much more quickly and eloquently than before.

These words are not universal to anxiety, but are universal to life.

Of course, knowing what I know now, anxiety was just the conduit for the learning. Your conduit could be anxiety, could be something else. No matter.

Life gives us . . . wait no, love gives us exactly what we need.

That does not mean shitty things happen for a reason. What it means is those shitty things happen and love takes them and turns them into opportunities for us to see light.

#ogreshavelayers
#sodoi

59
Take a Detour

"The shortest distance between two points
is a straight line.
If the two points are life and death,
why the heck would I want to go in a straight line?"

WE ALL HAVE A PLAN ON HOW WE THINK OUR life should unfold. And that is good, because it is important to have a clear understanding about where we want to go in life. However, sometimes you are put in a particular place because it was meant for your highest and best good. It may have not been what you have planned but it is exactly where you are supposed to be. Be open to it all. Know that life is not a straight line. When you are faced with a detour, embrace it with confidence. Fill yourself with the knowledge that you are being given the very things you need in your life at the exact moment you need to experience them. These detours will fill you with knowledge and the strength to move forward in the direction of your dreams and your destiny.

The same goes for healing. The straight line is most likely not going to happen. I wanted it to. I desperately wanted to blink in the *I Dream of Jeannie* way and be done with all the crap, but instead I seemed to be on the road to nowhere (thank you David Byrne).

It was in those difficult times I unearthed strength I had no idea I possessed.

It was in those difficult times I tapped into a faith that was beyond this world.

It was in those difficult times I reached out to connect.

It was in those difficult times I witnessed growth within myself.

#growth

#risingup

60
Crowd Out

"You have more power in the present moment
than in any other time in your life.
It's your move."

I LEARNED THAT MY POWER IS IN TODAY. PERI-
od.

I learned to let go of yesterday's pain.

I had a choice right now, today, to change the trajectory* of my life. And even if I chose not to do anything, I still had made a choice. (Can you hear the riff
of the Rush guitarist in your head right now?)

When I was caught up in anxiety, I lived day to
day asking "why me" and "how do I get out of this?"
It wasn't until I learned to let go of yesterday's suffering and truly believe in the present moment that my
transformation began.

I took control of what I could.

The control I had was my own personal perspective and intention.

The control I didn't have was what happened in the past or what was going to happen in the future.

I made no room for anxiety. It was like how nutritionists teach you to crowd out; you know when they tell you to eat an abundance of good nutritious food which will leave little room for the junk. Well, it is the same with anxiety. You crowd out anxiety by setting ambitious intentions and filling your mind with what you wish your life to look like right now. In this moment. This leaves very little room for the anxiety to take hold.

Even if I was experiencing panic attacks, I knew to let them happen but to give them no importance, as they were not what I wanted to carry into my tomorrow. I chose to believe the future did not have to include this type of suffering, and I counted the anxiety as a blessing, which was teaching me how to let go.

You have the opportunity every day to shift your intention to that which gives you peace. The fears of yesterday are not real, but illusions from the truth. As you begin today to create the life you want, you absolutely can move from a victim mentality to that of power and strength. You can begin to build positive moments, which in turn will align you with a progression of amazing days to follow. The results will astound you, as you continue to move forward in a positive light, seeing everything as a blessing.

We are ALL given the power to create. Choose not to think small or live in your past. Once you come to understand the enormity of power you possess, you

will clearly see how today is the day you created yesterday.

You have endless possibilities.

#powerful

#letgo

*God, I love the word trajectory. I really wanted to use it in
this book, so happy I found a place for it.

61
Fear or Love

"Every cell is listening.
What do you want them to hear?"

REMEMBER IN THE BOOK *HORTON HEARS A Who* when all the Whos were screaming from the wish flower, "We are here! We are here! We are here!??"

Your cells are creating a similar campaign for you to listen to them. This is because every cell in your body hears you and is trying to let you know it responds to what it hears. Obviously, the cells cannot talk to you like the Whos, but they do communicate. Their feedback is evident in your health.

I was taught that when you hold the vibration of love, your cells are open and receptive to nourishment and heath. However, the opposite is also true. If you hold yourself in the vibration of fear, your cells recoil, and close. Every cell in your body responds to your beliefs and thoughts about the world. Since you emanate these energetic messages from your positive and negative thoughts, you have the absolute power to create a state of balance in your mind, body and spirit.

Love yourself. Hold onto loving thoughts about the world and others.

If you have a negative thought (which we all do, thousands of times a day) do not hold on to it.

Accept the negative thought, let it go and give it zero importance.

When you create space for a self-love and love for others you become a force that nothing can permeate. This is because your entire body is on board with the love train and becomes a shield for sickness. You have so much power over your mental and physical reality.

#feedyourcells
#therightfood

62
Good Morning

"Every day is a fresh start.
Heck, every second is a new start."

EACH SUNRISE IS A NEW DAY. A BRAND-NEW start that holds infinite possibilities.

It is a great reminder of how I needed to learn from the past, but not live in it.

I had a past. We all do.

While much of our history may hold great memories, we have a tendency to carry around what was not so positive, and to let those memories, thoughts and beliefs hold us back. However, when we do that, when we carry our traumas and bad memories around, we are actually breathing life into that which we wish to release.

The past has only the power you give it. Nothing more.

Holding tightly to that which is no longer there, brings you more of what you don't want.

I had to learn let go of what no longer served me and instead create what I wanted in my life.

You have an opportunity at every moment to let go of all the illusions, and step into the greatness of what you truly are.

So, let's say or sing "Good Morning . . . Good Morning," (and if you wish to break out into dance with Gene Kelly okay) and embrace the newness of the day and your opportunity for letting go.

Remember, you cannot reach for anything new if your hands are full of yesterday's clutter.

#lettinggo

63
I Am Me

*"You are not your diagnosis.
The diagnosis is not you.
Believe. Rinse. Repeat."*

AT TIMES I WAS SO FAR GONE, I TRULY thought I was going to need to be hospitalized.

I had no idea what it all meant, and I placed *all* my trust in those that diagnosed me.

You see I bought into the fact that I was wrong.

That I was broken.

That I needed to be fixed.

I identified myself as my diagnoses.

I lived day to day in that existence and nothing got better. Of course, now I understand by holding space for the labels, I was asking the universe for more of what I already had.

It took time for me to get to where I am today, but one of the most important lessons for me was that my current health was not who I was, but instead was an indicator that it was time for change.

Change in my beliefs.

Change in my self-care.

Change in my perceptions.

Once I saw myself as lovingly perfectly imperfect, I understood that I was more powerful than I ever knew. I had the ability to change what I could, accept what I could not change, and love myself no matter what.

As my perceptions changed, the right people and circumstances appeared that helped me grow and heal in ways I never thought possible.

I am not perfect. I don't float around my house in balance every day.

I am human and deal with issues. We all do.

I just have made the conscious choice to know that I am love and perfection *in action.*

Thoughts and beliefs create reality.

#perfectlyimperfect

64
Say Hello to My Little Friend

"Healing is an inside job.
No one is coming to save you.
But you my friend, you can help yourself."

THIS WAS A TOUGH ONE FOR ME.

(As if there were any easy ones??)

It is 100% my job to get myself better.

Not my husband's, not my physician, energy heal-er, therapist, herbalist, friend, whomever, not their job. It is mine.

I went to every kind of person that I thought could fix me. I started with doctors and would be mad at them for not having the answers I needed to get well. And this began a many years long journey of hunting for the very person that would be able to rid me of anxiety, allergies and chemical sensitivities. With each one I met, in time, I found them to be under-educat-ed and I judged their abilities in their profession. For if they could not heal me, well, they must not be that good. Right?

Wrong. They were perfect in their roles. It was me that needed an adjustment.

I guess somehow, I thought I was entitled to a healing of my condition and that the power to help me was in someone else's hands. It was when I stopped playing victim and started being an active participant in my healing that things began to turn around.

I was not saying that others could not help:

I needed help.

I needed connection.

I needed others.

However, it was me that needed to do the work.

I made healing hard because I did not want to admit it was me that needed the adjustment. But when I did, life got so much better. And my prayers to God, even on a bad day changed from "Help Me" to "Thank You" because I learned all the healing is already here for us, we just have to believe and do what is needed to create the healing.

#ikindalikemenow

#thepoweriswithin

65
There is Enough

"It is safe to shine."

OTHER PEOPLE ARE NOT A THREAT TO YOUR goodness.

There is more than enough spotlight for everyone.

^ I had to learn this. Why? Because as a former perfectionist, the belief I held was that there is only room for number one. That just isn't true. I literally rewired my brain; first by letting go of the old belief and then repeating all the words below—every day.

Your time to shine is coming. Keep moving forward and enjoy healthy competition along the way. Those on your path are not there to knock you down, but to raise you up. Keep the right perspective, and it will all unfold perfectly for you.

It is easy to fall into the trap of believing you are not good enough, especially when we see others living their best and highest purpose. When we feel this way, lower vibrational feelings can emerge such as jealousy, anger, and sadness.

Someone's success can trigger you to begin comparisons, or a "them vs. me" mentality. You may even begin to doubt your own abilities because someone else has found success. This is particularly true when someone is successful in the field you believe is "yours." You may begin to believe that there is only room for so many, and you could possibly be squeezed out of the glory!

There is nothing further from the truth. You are unique and so is the gift you were born with. There is no one on this planet that can do the things you do exactly the way you do them. You are needed and your gift is not just for you, but to bring out to the world.

So be happy and rejoice in everyone's success stories. Remember, what you put out comes back to you. Therefore, when you are happy for others, truly happy for their success, you are a vibrational match for your own success.

It is like you are telling the universe:

There is enough for everyone.

I am happy for them and I will have some of mine now too please.

#shinebrightlikeadiamond

66
Secrets Make You Sick

"Throw it up, get it out.
It may be gross, but just think—
that was inside of you."

MANY OF US HAVE SOMETHING IN OUR PAST that we have hidden deep inside and wish no one to ever know. Or maybe something happened to you or you witnessed something that you keep a secret. Or maybe you are carrying around a burden that is not even yours. Even beliefs you affirm about yourself that are not a truth can keep you weighed down.

Keeping turbulent energy inside of me was making me sick. It was trapped energy.

This trapped energy wanted to get the fuck out.

When it was not allowed to leave, it sits. It festers.

By keeping everything inside I was hurting myself. Of course, I didn't know that but my body was trying to tell me.

The trapped energy became symptoms.

As the symptoms progressed, diseases were formed.

We are not meant to repress, but release what is not for our highest and best.

That is not to say we need to put our deepest information out on social media or shout from a rooftop about it. You can if you want, but letting it go is so much more.

You can write it out.

You can share with someone.

You can say prayers about it and ask God to hold it.

Whatever way you choose to release, know you are literally letting go of the secrets that hold you captive.

There is nothing that you *have* to carry inside.

You were never meant to be a container full of shit.

You are a vessel of love and kindness. Keep yourself clean inside and out.

#nooneisperfect

#weareallalittledirty

#getoutasmuchasyoucan

67
New Energy

"No one told me growth included outgrowth."

IN MY QUEST FOR UNDERSTANDING WHY I HAD anxiety and how I came out on the other side, I had to come to terms with a lot of misguided information I held within myself as my truth. The un-doing of false beliefs, engrained habits and unfounded fears was hard work. There was deep soul-searching that put me front and center of my own reflection, which put me in a position to face what I never wanted to see.

Me.

After many grueling years of improving my outlook and perspective about life and the world, I was able to look straight in the face of grief, anger, resentment and fear. Persevering fully in my goal of healing myself, I found a way to let go of the darkness that weighed me down and replace it with light.

I was a new woman. And I loved everything about myself. I was free. I grew . . .

What I was not prepared for was what I was out-growing. Of course, I knew the old beliefs and fear would be gone, I wanted to outgrow that. It was not the internal changes I was met with that concerned me, it was the outward changes.

You see by healing, my whole energy changed. I was no longer attracting those that saw me as wound-ed. Before I was carrying around a beacon call for help, and I latched onto certain people whom I admired. I took notes from these beautiful people and watched their moves, for I knew they were the ones I could learn from. They were my tribe. They were warriors. They were amazing.

When I healed though, we were no longer close. I felt abandoned and lost without them. I grieved for the loss of my friends. There were many lonely days and months that sometimes made me feel like my growth was a mistake. I went back over what I had done to create the rift and it was then I was able to see a new pattern emerge. A friend-shift. I had changed. They may have too. I was not sure. But we were definitely in different places. What we once had in common was no longer there. This is when I began to understand the famous friendship quote that said friends enter your life for a reason, a season or a lifetime. They were there at a time when I needed them and they needed me. And when that reason or season was complete, we parted ways.

The universe, God, whatever name you give love, has such a bigger plan in place than we could ever know. For when I let go and gave it to God *and* trusted

He knew what needed to be done, that is when new friends and opportunities began showing up in my life. It was miraculous. When I made the room, they were there.

It was also beautiful to witness some of the people that fell away from me reappear in my life to begin a new chapter together. I trust the process.

It was hard letting go.

It is still hard letting that be.

I love my new people

I grieve the old friends.

#growingup

#growingout

#growingin

68
The Happy Train

*"To be happy all the time
would be so exhausting, right?"*

HAPPINESS.

Everywhere I looked there was someone telling me how to be happy.

If you get in shape, you will be happy.

If you eat chocolate it makes you happy.*

If you have friends you are happier.

If you do what you love, you are happy.

But sometimes I wasn't happy. Even when I did everything that promised happiness.

The message clearly was I needed to do something immediately to *become* happy otherwise consequences . . . I am assuming the consequence was to be unhappy?

In our happy obsessed society, I had to break away and think it was okay not to be happy all the time. It actually is quite creepy to have a smile on your face 24/7; it reminds me of a clown with a painted smile.

Happy all the time is kind of a crappy expectation, because if you are not part of the club, you may think something is wrong. I know I did. But God certainly did not make us with an entire range of emotions to only feel one.

Happy is an emotion.

So is sadness. Anger. Grief. Fear.

I became cool with me no matter what emotion was coming up.

I felt it and then let it go.

I learned not to sit in the lower emotions, but also not to be upset by them.

And when happiness came, I greeted it openly and allowed it to stay as long as it wanted.

We are not just happy beings.

We are human beings.

#itsokay
#tbh
#iammostlyhappy
#butnotallthetime
#andidonthaveaclownsmile
#Iactuallyhave
#restingbitchface

*it does lol

69
Take Out the Garbage

"Allowing in the negative pollutes the soul."

IT IS SO VERY EASY TO FALL INTO THE TRAP OF negativity. It is everywhere, from the moment you wake, to the moment you shut your eyes. And even when you try to fall asleep, the events of your day will replay in your head before you drift off for the night.

When I was suffering with anxiety, I took stock of what I let into my day:

- negative people
- negative news
- negative thoughts
- negative food
- negative gossip
- negative activities
- negative time (excess phone and computer time)

The above list was an eye opener as to why my anxiety would flare up day after day. It is not to say these things were the *cause* of my anxiety, but they certainly contributed to the *increase* in symptoms. I had to let go of the negative and find what was positive. This is tough for a person with an anxiety condition, because we tend to focus on what could go wrong and believe that holding onto the bad somehow makes it go away. Nothing could be further from the truth. Letting go of the negative made room for all that was good.

At first it was difficult to find good, so I began with small steps. A gratitude list helped. I was literally changing the direction of my life by changing what I chose to focus on. Focusing upon the good let up on the constant flight or fight surging through my system, and my nervous system was able to calm down.

There was no need to repeatedly watch or listen to negative all day long.

What you fill your mind with is what your brain believes you love.

Your connection to the universe is beautiful and will give more of what you focus on.

#positive

#or

#pollution?

70
Law of Thirds

"Do they like me? Is not the question.
Do you like you? That is the one to answer."

SOME OF THE BEST ADVICE I EVER GOT WAS this:

Not everyone likes you, so stop wasting your time on those that don't.

His unofficial science was this: approximately one-third of everyone likes you, one-third of people do not like you and the last third really don't have an opinion or care.

When I was younger, I worried when I felt that I was not being liked and I bent over backwards to get them to like me. What I did not understand at the time was this: I couldn't have ever done enough to get them to like me. It wasn't personal, it just was. I have since learned that our energy attracts certain people to help us at very specific points in our lives, and that is okay. But more importantly, to waste energy on those that don't like us is an exercise in futility. It is not your job to win them over, it is your job to listen to the angels around you that are supporting you and lifting you higher. Also, the more you obsess in their dislike, the more you lose a piece of yourself and your power.

I learned to not compromise myself for anyone.

I took back my power.

As you live grounded in your authentic self, there will be those that do not like you. Okay and good. That means you are taking a position and living a genuine life instead of a victim role of a people pleaser. Bless them and move on. They are there to show you that their path is not your life path and we can all walk different roads and still live fully, vibrating love for all.

#lawofthirds

#itsokay

#rightpeoplearethere

71
Going Fishing?

"I used this more than anything else in helping me overcome anxiety."

HONESTLY. THESE WORDS WERE ON MY FOLD-ed-up piece of paper in my pocket for years. These words were part of my anchor list.

It was on the screensaver of my phone and computer.

It was what my husband told me when I looked lost and couldn't get out of the rabbit hole on my own.

What was this magical phrase?

Don't take the bait.

Four of the most beautiful words that were my secret weapon against anxiety.

We know a fish taking the bait is a process of luring them with food, the same happens in our lives. We are lured in by our fears, our thoughts, other people's opinions, gossip and drama. Since we understand we cannot control our thoughts, and we certainly cannot control other people, we can choose to not take the bait.

I had no idea how to get myself out of the crippling thoughts that haunted me. These thoughts would fill my mind, and I would try endlessly to fight them, which caused even more adrenalin. The more I struggled to free myself, the worse the anxiety symptoms became. It was like pouring gasoline onto an already blazing fire. I was lost, sad and hopeless. I truly believed the rest of my life would be just battle after battle, trying to tame this monster, that consumed my every moment.

Then, one night, when my stomach was churning, and I felt the burning of another familiar panic attack coming on, I thought, let me try something different. I began an internal dialogue with myself. I reasoned, how about instead of fighting and fear, why don't I try acceptance and peace?

As I lay with my eyes open that evening, trying what was clearly counter intuitive to my survival skills, I let the panic wash over me, and did not react. The thoughts became stronger, and the physical symptoms more pronounced, trying their hardest to scare me into a reaction. I sat still, and just accepted them, as they crashed harder and harder upon my body and my mind. Then, this phrase popped into my mind "Don't take the bait." I smiled as this came forth, as I knew it was my new mantra. I learned not to take the bait of thoughts or physical symptoms.

I understood that many anxiety symptoms were just manifestations of stress, and as I let them be there, they would reduce. I learned to accept the fact that there will constantly be bait in the water, but I had the ability to swim around it and not hook on. I was mastering my peace.

#swimaroundit

#mantra

#power

72
Acceptance

"The key to healing is acceptance.
The lock is you."

ONE OF THE BIGGEST LESSONS I HAD TO LEARN was acceptance.

In fact, in every energy healing modality I learned, the bottom line to the healing was to accept everything and yourself just as you are.

^ Thank me later I just saved you about $10k in certifications.

I was always blaming others for what was happening to me. I was also blaming others when they couldn't "fix" me. I allowed them to be the stars in my life story. And because I gave them the power in my life, I was not able to make changes.

We have all had less than fortunate experiences in our lives. Some things go all the way back to childhood or just as recent as yesterday. Some of these struggles were traumatic, but unfortunately, we cannot turn back the clock. We have zero control over others and what happened. We do have control of how we react and how we wish it to shape us going forward.

The moment you accept everything the way it is right now is the moment you can change and grow. You are empowered when YOU take life by the reins and choose consciously which direction you wish to go.

I had to let go of blaming anyone or anything for my situation. The past is gone. I let it go.

Keeping myself locked in the past, did nothing but hurt me and keep me stuck. Taking responsibility and acceptance for my life put the power to change where it was always meant to be—with me.

Acceptance was the key. Forgiveness is the lock.

When I allowed both in, the doors for healing opened.

#accepteverything
#eventhesymptoms
#springboardforchange
#gamechanger

73
God Has Got This

"Thank you. I couldn't hold it all."

I CAN CLEARLY REMEMBER THE MOMENT someone told me to put it all in God's hands. This was a cause for extreme anxiety for me. I actually can recall shaking for 24 hours straight (no exaggeration) worrying about this. Why? Because a large part of anxiety is control. And to relinquish control, to give it away, was a scary option. I believed that I had to hold it all. I guess I believed this because I thought if I held it all, then I had control over it. What I did not understand at the time is I really never had control.

To be honest, I was scared of God. I was also pretty mad at Him. But I took the step to examine my relationship with Him. It began with me changing my religion. I thought God and my religion were synonymous. I thought by changing religions I was going to solve everything. My new church was amazing and welcoming. I learned so much about community and love. But I soon realized my church is not responsible for my relationship with God, I was. My church was a place to go to honor that relationship. But I still was not ready to give up control.

So, the next thing I did was to dive into learning more about God. I read the Bible. Not just the one I had, but I also read children versions, and books about the Bible. I read and joined discussion groups in *The Course of Miracles*. I actually led discussion groups in my church to teach about this book. But even still, I was not ready to fully give up control.

I began to listen to Christian rock and I really liked it. The words were so uplifting and made me feel so incredible. The lyrics were in my mind when I felt a panic attack coming on. If the lyrics did not work, I would use Scripture to help me overcome anxiety. I still have the crinkled piece of loose-leaf paper that has Bible verses written on it to help me with fear, anxiety, frustration, sickness and depression.

Even with all of this, I held onto control.

And after a few years trying to iron out my relationship with God, I finally understood what I needed to do. I needed to let go *and* also get out of God's way. He had a plan and it did not need my interference. My job was to accept and allow. This would take trust. This would take faith. Two things I had lost very early in life and without them I was a perfect candidate for anxiety. I realized that anxiety may have many spokes for why it was in my life (diet, hormones, stress, habits etc.) but there was a foundational reason—a center— that created the environment for those spokes to take hold. And my reason was I did not trust and I had little faith.

In the past I would have tried to fix this myself, but in that moment, I asked God. No, I actually thanked God in advance for healing me from not just anxiety, but my lack of trust and faith. It was here, in this space of trust, that I felt a huge load be lifted from my shoulders. It was not a spontaneous healing. God had greater plans for me in the form of lessons, of interactions, of friendships and opportunities. I learned that anxiety was my gift. That because of it, I healed the wounds that created lack of trust and faith. I also was given the ability to write about it and help others. I finally gave up control. Well, I really never had it, but He waited patiently until I figured that out.

My faith game is strong. And because of that I am strong. It is not of me, but through me that I have healed. No matter what you call God . . . love, the universe, source . . . it is the solid force that feeds you everything, that is always there for you, that loves you. Tap into that energy. That love. It is waiting for you.

#faith
#trust
#miracles

74
These Thoughts

*"Just because you have a thought
doesn't mean it is true."*

THOUGHTS INVADE THE MIND OF THE ANX-
ious and stressed brain. I knew my *job* was to calm my
brain in order to let go of anxiety, but I did not know
how, until I understood what thoughts truly were.

The definition of a thought is this: "an idea or opinion produced by thinking or occurring suddenly in the
mind." Notice that the description does not mention
a thought as a fact or an absolute, it says an opinion.
An idea.

Just because you have a thought, does not make it
true. This means to accept all thoughts as they come,
but you do not have to believe them.

I began to slowly understand this and tried not
to tie any energy into negative thoughts. I did this by
not giving them attention. This taught my brain that
these thoughts were not important. Without attention

they simply dissolved into nothingness. And when I had a positive thought, I gave all my energy to it, and allowed those thoughts to expand in my mind.

I had to learn whatever I resist becomes stronger. What I hold onto, grows.

Thoughts are not bad or good.

They just are. They are meaningless.

Until *I choose* to grab onto them and give them meaning.

#justathought

#notatruth

#power

75
It's in the Genes

"Breaking the hurts of the past
clear way for the future."

THIS WAS SOME SUPER FREAKY SHIT TO ME.

When I learned about generational issues I was blown away.

Of course, I knew about getting your eye color or weird pinky toe passed down generation to generation, but I never thought about the emotional stuff being passed down!

I blindly accepted not just the physical but emotional lineage as my truth, because I never took the time to examine it. And even when I did, I felt powerless to change.

Just like eye color is inherited, so too are the emotional traumas of our ancestors, the ones that were never healed. These traumas can show up in both emotional and physical forms. Pain can travel through families and it continues to be passed down from generation to generation UNTIL someone in the family is ready and brave enough to heal it themselves.

To be honest, at the time, I really was hesitant to do this work, it seemed too woo-woo. I prayed. And the answer I received was that healing comes in many forms. However, I was not prepared for how quickly some of the "heaviness" in my life was instantly lifted when I addressed these issues. It was crazy!

I am sure there are many ways to heal these generational issues. First that comes to mind is prayer. I know there are many forms of energy healing that also hone in on generational issues. I believe that energy healing is just prayer in action, so I was able to bring my faith and the energy healing together, knowing it all comes through me, not of me.

I first had to see how these generational issues were serving me? And then how to heal these traumas across the generational lines. It was interesting and beautiful. By going through the pain of healing, I realized I will no longer pass this poison and burden to my children.

We are so beautiful and powerful.

#breakinguptheband

76
Groundhog Day

"For circumstances to change,
you have to take the action to make a change."

I HAVE NO IDEA WHY I LIVED THERE—IN THE
pain—but I did.

I would relive it over and over until one day a woman helping me told me this:

> "The first time you live through it,
> it is on them and/or the problem.
> Every other time you re-live this, it is on you."

WOW! The way I interpreted her statement was
you lived through the traumas once. And you were
hurt. And it is not your fault. That is the only time you
need to live through it. Any other time you bring it up,
it is *you* hurting *you*. *They* are no longer hurting you
because it is over. *The problem* no longer can hurt you
because it was years ago.

This is a very simple statement that seems to be an almost overwhelming task to overcome.

But when I thought about it in these terms, it became so apparent that it was my job to get the help and the tools to address the issue and let it go, but never my job to hold it forever.

I refused to keep breathing life into what I no longer wanted.

I instead made the choice to breathe life into what I wanted my future to look like.

I was no longer going to allow anyone or anything that happened to steal my joy.

I took back my power. I forgave. I moved forward.

Being healthy was my new goal, not getting rid of anxiety. Getting rid of anxiety was not my goal because using the energy of the *word anxiety* kept me stuck in the goopy, nasty beliefs of the past. Getting healthy was a shiny new way of looking at it.

I was not allowing anything, even old beliefs, to steal my time any longer.

#healthy

#thatwasmygoal

#stillis

#areyoustillreadingthese?

#justchecking

77
There's a Party
in my Tummy

"What you feed yourself is everything.
Thoughts. Food. Faith."

THIS WOULD NOT BE A COMPLETE BOOK UNTIL I talked about nutrition.

Nutrition was one of the top three things I absolutely needed in order to heal from anxiety.

I didn't want to believe it. Many times, I fought it.

I mean I cannot say enough about how much I love chocolate.

But for my particular healing, sugar had to go away for a long while. I eat it now but nothing like I did. Gluten took a hike. So did coffee and caffeine. Dairy I only eat in small amounts.

That is not nutrition though. Giving up certain foods does not constitute healthy eating.

It was a start. And letting go of those foods brought me light years away from symptoms.

Some of it was so dramatic that I saw results overnight.

My lesson though was not what I gave up, but what I was putting in.

What was I eating on a daily basis? How did that make me feel?

There were lots of experiments and reactions. Finally, I found a great balance that worked for me.

Obviously loads of vegetables. I mean loads. But even then, do what works for you.

Like the cauliflower craze is on, and to be honest I don't feel well eating it. All good. Good for some, not for all. I moved on. In addition to veggies, fruit works great for me. So does some protein. So do carbs. Wait? Did I say carbs??? Yes. For me it is a must do. The carbs work so well for my brain and helps it function properly. May not work for you though. Everyone has their own repertoire of healing foods.

The gut-brain connection information was such a saving grace for me and still is. I love learning about how nutrition helps the brain function. Good food is the fuel I needed to help me heal.

#foodforthought

78
Get Outside and Go

"Exercise was and still is a lifeline for me."

I CANNOT BEGIN TO STRESS THIS ENOUGH.

I want to shout it from rooftops.

If you are dealing with anxiety, exercise is your best friend.

I can end this lesson here.

But I won't. I like writing and hearing the tap-tap-tap of the keyboard.

Seriously. Exercise was profound to my healing.

My goal was to get out every day and do *something*.

Anything. The symptoms reduced significantly when I began a regular exercise routine.

I found what worked for me and stuck with it. I walked.

I was like Forest Gump, walking all day long. Okay exaggeration, but I did walk every day.

I tried many other forms of exercise, but I kept coming back to loving just a nice walk.

I also began meditating. I first began this when I had really bad panic attacks. I would just sit with myself and breathe. Then it turned into mediating every night before bed. Before long I was mediating in the mornings. It was a lifeline for sure.

No matter the exercise or relaxation technique you choose, choose!

Today if I feel my stress levels rising and my barrel getting full, I know to get out and take a walk. And to follow it up with deep breathing and a chill out meditation.

#walkandmeditate

#peasandcarrots

79
Setbacks

*"Recovery. Recovery. Setback. Recovery.
Yeah, that is about how it went."*

RECOVERY BEGAN SLOWLY.

I wanted it all immediately. Sometimes I only felt better for minutes at a time.

However, in time the minutes turned into hours and then days of relief.

There were days that I would sleep through the night and I would wake thrilled that I was actually once again getting restorative sleep.

That is why the first setback hit me so hard.

It was such a blow to my confidence.

I got so mad. How dare the anxiety come back after all the work I had done?

After a few days I would again feel better. But without fail maybe a week or a month later I was brought back into the world I wanted so desperately out of.

These setbacks were devastating to me. And I would react horribly to them.

My lesson was to see the setback in a new light.

I started to see them as opportunities. It allowed me to measure how far I had come. I learned if they bothered me so much, it was because there were really good days and weeks before the setback. I had a gratitude journal that I could look back in and see progress made. It was astonishing how far I had come. The setback was merely a rest stop, a break in the healing that allowed me to look around and be grateful for my progress.

It is okay to take a few steps back. It is part of the anxiety dance.

Bless the setback and

don't stop believin'.

^I love that song. Made it my anthem. Never stop believing.

#holdontothatfeelin

#whatajourney

#dontcallitasetback

#callitasetup

#forhealing

80
Imperfect

"No one is immune to imperfection."

YOU READ MY STORY.

What I didn't tell you is that even though I knew I needed to avoid certain foods and products; I was not perfect in following the restrictions. And even today while I consider myself healed from the terrible symptoms; I take liberties sometimes that are definitely not in my best interest.

Healed is a funny word sometimes.

Actually, now that I write this, I don't find it funny at all, but see it as a deceiving word. Is anyone ever healed? What I mean is I always thought healed meant all done, finished, nothing more to see here. (That's all folks!) But really healing means changing what you can and accepting what you can't.

I thought healed meant I could eat and drink whatever I wanted.

But I realized that would be ridiculous. We are not

made to thrive on junk food and toxins all around us. Even though I am healed from anxiety, I know I have a responsibility to myself to stay on top of my health, eating well and exercising.

We all have our own personal limits. I like the analogy of the overflowing barrel to show how our body reacts when we exceed our limits. Imagine this barrel is full of anxiety, environmental stressors, nutritional choices, family issues, etc. This barrel can only handle so much before it overflows, and when it does symptoms and even diseases begin to surface. Our job, so to speak, is to reduce the level in our barrel. When we do symptoms begin to subside.

Sometimes I don't heed the warning of my barrel getting ready to overflow and I get symptoms. So yes, I am healed. No, I am not immune to the issues we all are when our barrel overflows.

The good news is, I now know I am not stuck. I can get out of it. I take responsibility for getting into the mess, which gives me the position of power to get out of it. While I am very unhappy dealing with symptoms, I know they are temporary and a beautiful sign from my body telling me to please stop. I help myself by mediating a bit more, getting off my phone, eating the foods that my body craves for health and forgiving myself for what happened.

While it is not recommended to go off the rails of healing, it does happen. I have lovingly told myself it's okay. What a beautiful body, mind, and soul I have to give me opportunities to be well.

Thank yourself if you find yourself in this position.

Your body is so kind to communicate with you and let you know what it needs.

#setbacks
#partofthestory
#eatingthatchocolatebarwasgoodthough
#backtoveggies

81
Sharing Your Smile

*"Helping others once you have helped
your inside shine is the best feeling ever."*

I HAVE ALWAYS TRIED TO BE KIND. HOWEVER, I am human and therefore absolutely certain that there were times that I was not being the best version of myself. But all and all, I believe that kindness is our natural human state and that all of our life compasses are set on sharing smiles. I think it is so much harder to be a dick than to be kind. It really does take more energy to be mean, and it is effortless to be nice, right?

There are so many ways you can share your smile. The most obvious is to be kind.

A smile. A kind word. A helping hand.

Kindness expands.

If we were all kind; could you imagine what this world would be like?

It is like a ripple effect. You know what I mean, like when you toss a rock into the ocean and the rock hits the water at a center point. And from that point, a ripple expands outwards in all directions. Your kind gesture; be it a smile or a kind word is that center point and expands out into the world just like a ripple.

And while anxious, I know sometimes it is hard to be Sally Sunshine, but please try. Because anxiety wins if you turn inwards and separate yourself from the connection of the world. You were never meant to be isolated, that is anxiety's trick, don't fall for it. You are meant to be plugged into the goodness and the light.

All that we think, say and do has an effect on everyone. You have the ability to make changes, with simple actions, which will create energy to move in the direction of your action.

Be the light that expands the energy of this world to a higher vibration. As you do this, others will as well. It is contagious. As we all begin to share our smiles, the collective consciousness of kindness grows to outlandish proportions.

And just like with all in life; the kindness you send out comes back to you.

You can change the world. You are that amazing. You may believe you are just one drop in the ocean, but always remember what one drop can do.... and the energetic influence you can have on it all.

#powerfulasshit

#kindnessrocks

82
Why the Name?

"Love Always, Lucie.
It was so simple, but profound."

WE ALL HAVE BEEN THROUGH TRIALS AND tribulations. My story is no different than yours, except in the details. I said in the beginning of this book and I am saying it again: we are more alike than we are different.

You have read how I wrestled with anxiety for close to 15 years. Panic attacks were a daily occurrence, and at times sleep was a luxury. I was a prisoner in my home and at one point my 5-foot 9-inch frame was weighing in at about one hundred pounds.

This is what I said was wrong with me.

So, how did I try to get myself right?

I tried medication, talk therapy, energy healing, nutritional healing, vitamin therapy, acupuncture, exercise, hypnotherapy, hydrotherapy (still makes me giggle). I flew around the country to top specialists, and spent lots of money on the most cutting-edge alternative treatments. Many of these helped for a short time, but did not completely fix what I wanted to be changed. I was looking to fight this condition until I won. However, once I learned to accept everything, to put down the sword and stop fighting, is when true healing began.

But it really does not matter what I have been through. What matters more is what I have left behind.

I left behind the lies and deceit, not from others but from my own self. For years I was internally repeating words and thoughts that stuck and took hold in my mind. In my body. In my life. It was these beliefs that needed to be kicked out and replaced with new, updated thoughts and patterns. Sometimes we don't even know we hold these thoughts and beliefs, as they can be deep rooted from many years ago.

As I let the lies go, I brought in goals, dreams and purpose. I allowed myself to believe in the power of goodness and love. I learned to feed my soul the right food, which also included feeding my body nutritious meals. And as I did, my life changed and continues to change.

I had been searching all those years for an answer to my suffering and the answer was within me all along. Unconditional love is the foundation from which all the other lessons could take hold.

When you truly understand that you are love and you move through life as love you vibrate at such a high frequency that lights you up and allows you to see all else was an illusion.

And that is why I named my blog Love Always, Lucie. It is a reminder to always love myself always no matter what. And when you learn to love yourself no matter what; anxiety has zero hold on you.

#lovewins

83
The Anxious Hippie

*"When you come full circle with fresh eyes
The blessings can be viewed everywhere."*

YES, I AM QUITE AWARE ANXIOUS HIPPIE IS A contradiction.

Healing from anxiety is also a contradiction of sorts. Why?

A couple reasons:

First is because the way out of anxiety is counter intuitive to what you believe you need to do. I mean honestly it is bizarre; your body says fight but really, you need to just sit there and chill. It is such a difficult thing to master, but once you get the hang of it you can begin to see the humor in the paradox. There never needed to be a fight. It was a challenge that you need not have accepted. When you learn to lay down your sword and smile in the face of the fear; you win. Unfortunately (or fortunately) for me it took many battles to learn that.

Second, because anxiety ultimately teaches you so much about yourself. It is beautiful to learn that from pain and darkness can come light and freedom. And you learn that it is those dark places that cultivated the seeds for change and growth. Would I have wished to grow without all the pain?? Of course! But would I have grown into who I am today without that pain? Probably not. Because there would not have been a reason to reach so far down within myself and pull out what was needed to overcome and break free.

And lastly anxiety is a contradiction because without it, I would not have found me. The true me that was hiding behind everything else. Anxiety forced me to take a good look at myself, straight in the mirror, and see me. Not the person I was pretending to be. And when I truly saw who was there, I happily embraced her. I now lovingly honor the time that I was anxious. Not because it was fucking spectacular to suffer like I did, but because it was through the gift of anxiety that I was forced to look; and then to love.

The anxious hippie is not a label, but more so my life song. It is a way to show that life itself is a contradiction and to flow one way or the other is merely a fluid motion that only needs acceptance by me. Anxious is cool; for I know there must be more lessons to uncover. Hippie is cool because it is my true self exposed. It is that alignment with my soul and my outer self that makes it all of this worth it. What a blessing this crazy ride has been.

Part 4

Peace of Mind

"Helping one another
See the light."

I was once asked by a group
That had invited me to speak
How can we help people understand anxiety?
I smiled and said.
"You. By sharing and helping them see."
The most beautiful words at that moment were spoken.

84
Now You Know

"Bringing light to where things need to be seen."

There is no one way anxiety begins. If you are dealing with anxiety, your way is unique to you (or your loved one). That is why it is so very difficult that we use one only word to describe it-

Anxiety.

It could be something from childhood.
It could be a trauma from adulthood.
It could be you just have a low tolerance for stress.
It could be too much stress.
It could contribute to a medical issue.
It could be your diet or lack of exercise.
It could be nutritional deficiencies.
It could be just be fear. Of failure. Of love. Of
    spiders . . . anything.
Maybe you were born with a predisposed condition

that creates anxiety.
It could be grief in disguise.
It could be boundary issues.
It could be any number of reasons.

I do know anxiety is your body talking to you, giving
    you feedback.
It took time for me to listen.
Listening and learning were the keys to
    understanding.

I began to listen to me . . .

You may be a friend or someone I just know casually.
You may even be family or someone I have worked
    with in the past.
Or someone who is suffering now with anxiety,
    reading this book.
No matter how.
We are connected, we *met* for a purpose.
I truly believe that.
You were placed before me, and I before you
For reasons we may never understand.
It was orchestrated well before you picked up this
    book.
The crossings are never by chance
We give one another something that is needed to
    propel us into our future self
We may associate negative or positive emotions
    towards one another
But we are all angels in disguise.

The good or the bad of any relationship is our own
    fabrication
Because if we look deep enough,
We can see that each of us has a role, a mission
Which brings each other strength, opportunity and
    growth.
It can bring boundaries, a voice and action.
Whatever the reason, the lesson is there and for us to
    explore.

For years I struggled with extreme anxiety and
    sensitivity.
I wanted to shed my skin and deny myself.
Because I could not understand why me?
Why was I was plagued with this disease?
And why was it I that suffered,
To the level of extremity that it was.
It was an albatross I could not cut loose from.
I fought it and battled it until I was tired and weak.
Its strength frightened me and made me feel less
    than.

I would wear a smile or break out in laughter.
To feel included and belong.
Accepted.
But when I retreated to deal with my demons
And isolated myself to heal,
Many left my side
A few strong warriors stayed.
I don't blame you.
You didn't understand.

What I do know now is that not only were you
    teaching me,
But I you.

The invisible illnesses need to be seen
We need to find a way to be able to
Crack open the mystery of what is going on inside.

If someone has a broken leg,
We see the injury.
It is visible.
We give people the time and the space to heal.
We cheer them as they progress.
Cast being removed.
Rehabilitation
And movement.
We love them through it
And understand that they may need
Help, love and understanding.
We give that and don't judge.

If someone has cancer,
We are hurt
Because we do not want our friend or family
To be hurting.
It is devastating.
It is visible.
We support and love them.
We cheer for them as they
Do brave things to get well.
These are warriors in and of themselves.

We love them through it
And understand that they may need
Help, love and understanding.
We give that and don't judge.

If someone has anxiety
You cannot see it.
It is somewhat misunderstood.
You may feel bad for your friend
But the expectation is not the same
As a visible illness.
Because the hurt is not quantifiable.
It can't be measured.
And because we all have had stress
We can only equate it to what we have known.
And what you have known may have only been
A drop in the bucket to another's.

So, the highly anxious person
Trudges on with life.
Trying to appear normal on the outside,
While inside they are very sick
And breaking down inside.
They don't have the rest
Or the support
Because it is not apparent to others
What is needed.
They do not know.

This creates a battle with the self
That makes them feel weak

Or less than
Because they are seen as
"Just having anxiety".
And to move on with it.
And they can't.
It is not possible.
We **need** to love them through it.
And understand that they may need
Help, love and understanding.
We **need** to give that and **not** judge.

I know my role was to write this story.
And you were meant to read my story.
To crack open the truth and resolve the mystery
Of what is inside.
To see where eyes cannot see.
And find the compassion and connection
For those wanting so badly to heal.

And you, you are a helper.
And can spread the message on.
Thank you.

#passiton
#thankyou
#helponeanother

About the Author

Lucie Dickenson is beach loving light-seeker, who truly believes anxiety can be your greatest blessing. She is an anxiety helper, stigma squasher, perspective darer and a chocolate freak. Lucie also has a very unique snort when she laughs; that she has learned to embrace fully.

To learn more about Lucie visit her website
www.luciedickenson.com.

Lucie invites you to check out the soon to be released *The Anxious Hippie Handbook.* It is a fun workbook and journal that takes you through all the lessons in *The Anxious Hippie.* It is like having your own personal roadmap to guide you in finding peace, love and the blessings in anxiety.

CPSIA information can be obtained
at www.ICGtesting.com
Printed in the USA
LVHW020923040820
662292LV00016B/468